UNTO THIS LAST

and

TRAFFIC

For Gerald
who also likes
Kids.

J. R.

JOHN RUSKIN

Unto this Last
and
Traffic

EDITED BY
John L. Bradley
UNIVERSITY OF SOUTH CAROLINA

New York
APPLETON-CENTURY-CROFTS
Division of Meredith Publishing Company

PRINTED IN THE UNITED STATES OF AMERICA
E 23329

CONTENTS

INTRODUCTION

When John Ruskin wrote the articles that would comprise *Unto this Last*[1] in the summer of 1860, he had been the aesthetic arbiter of middle-class Victorian England for more than a decade. Many triumphs lay behind him. He had recently completed the fifth volume of *Modern Painters*, a sprawling, brilliantly provocative work, initiated as far back as 1843, when its author had just come down from Oxford to revolutionize the world of art. He had also published *The Seven Lamps of Architecture*, a stimulating and sometimes strident book bursting with unorthodox ideas and purporting to do for the glories of building what *Modern Painters* was effecting for art. But Ruskin had accomplished even more, for between 1851 and 1853 he produced the three volumes of *The Stones of Venice,* a sweeping masterpiece that is an extraordinary amalgam of sociological investigation and architectural enquiry into Venetian tombs, churches, and palazzi, as well as an eloquent moral document that illustrates the rise and fall of a civilization in terms of its artistic representation. *The Stones* combines, as no other work of Ruskin's, those emotionally charged, colorfully expressed, idiosyncratic yet weightily perceptive ideas, loosely termed Ruskinian. Furthermore, during the years before 1860 Ruskin lectured end-

[1] Matthew 20:14.

vii

lessly, evaluated hundreds of pictures for galleries and museums, and acted as artistic cicerone to rising businessmen who wished to purchase entry to the upper middle classes; he also gave generously of his services to the growing Working Men's College, an enterprise designed to encourage the education of the less privileged. Thus by the age of forty Ruskin succeeded— and it may well be his supreme achievement—in conveying to the middle classes the importance of a standard of taste in aesthetic matters. And through lectures, letters (public and private), and extended passages of rolling prose within his longer works, he posited the necessity for social change. His accomplishment was immense; and it still reverberates through the chaotic uproar of twentieth-century life.

Thus Ruskin's path to *Unto this Last,* although it may seem to lie primarily in the labyrinth of aestheticism, was marked by various signposts that suggest social and economic concerns and point to his growing interest in formulating a theory of political economy. Indeed, if one plots a graph of Ruskin's work from beginning to end, the years prior to 1860 stand out in their adherence to the shaping of artistic canons— canons that are inextricably connected, however, with subordinated social concerns. Then, after the social concerns reach their supreme articulation in *Unto this Last,* a leveling off follows for the remainder of his long life in which the world of art and the world of social concern remain in relative equilibrium. For while the last half of Ruskin's span is a tragic complex of blighted love, futile aspiration, and thwarted hope, his work, which became bafflingly diffuse and fragmented with the years, does, ironically, have a direction in which the twin movements of the social and the artistic move together and with comparable emphases.

Ruskin pronounced his ideas on political economy against an extremely hostile background, for his beliefs ran counter to the economical theories that obtained in England during the high Victorian years. The exponents of these concepts—for instance, Adam Smith and David Ricardo, John Stuart Mill (later to modify his position)—adhered to the principle of *laissez-faire,* a polite term for ruthless competition uncontrolled by governmental interference. They further believed that if the basic laws of supply and demand operate without hindrance, the riches of the country must inevitably proliferate. They saw wealth itself as no more than an accumulation of material things and that tragic figure, "economic man," as a bloodless abstraction bereft of human sentiment. They were oblivious to the necessity of fraternal bonds between members of a changing society, and under the guise of enlightened self-interest, they held that the individual was the best judge of where that interest lay—not surprisingly, it generally reposed within his own acquisitive bosom. Their ideas ran riot through Victorian England at a time when people were flocking to the towns from the country to make their living in the fast-rising mills and factories. As a result, a huge population of underpaid, underfed, undereducated men, women, and children toiled in these centers of productivity at sub-starvation wages; and as fast as their exploiters became wealthy, these unfortunate people were driven to starvation, drunkenness, disease, prostitution, and, in short, utter degradation. From the atrocities of these years, however, came much literature of protest. In 1843, with Carlyle's *Past and Present*, the position of the oppressed in this new, painfully forming industrial order was eloquently, even prophetically, set forth. Soon after came Disraeli's *Sybil* (appropriately subtitled *The Two Nations,* that is, the rich and the poor), a cumbersome but sincere attempt to define the chasm between oppressor and oppressed. And Mrs. Gaskell's *Mary Barton,* an intense narrative exposing the filth and squalor of northern industrial life, is a memorable testimony to the inadequacy of relations between employer and employed. A few years later, in 1854, Dickens published *Hard Times,* an indignant exposition of middle-class commercial competition and its disastrous outcome in poverty, alcoholism, and early death. A carefully plotted, economical masterpiece, *Hard Times* is a stinging indictment of the deification of fact at the expense of human feeling and of predatory individualism at the cost of Christian charity. Like *Mary Barton,* the novel explicates the failure in communication between employer and workman—the absence, that is, of "social affection." In addition, as the industrial rapacity gathered momentum, humanitarian magazines and newspapers took up the cry by exposing the dens of vice and warrens of profligacy that spread like a malign growth through the large cities of the country, especially in the north. By the time Ruskin wrote *Unto this Last* the predicament of the poor, in spite of ameliorative efforts, was a national disgrace.

Despite all the documentation available on Ruskin's life, we know little about his social conscience during his earliest years; but as a younger man his reading suggests an awakening to questions of social import. Shortly thereafter, in *The Seven Lamps of Architecture,* he inquires into the mental state of the workman;

how happy, he asks, is the stonecarver? Was his work "done with enjoyment"? He reminds us that the feelings, the deeper concerns of the craftsman, are of signal importance, for if the man dislikes his work and is thankful when it is completed, then the results will be "dead as leaves in December." Ruskin avers that payment, a cash basis to a relationship, is not enough: "money will not buy life." This is soon followed by the pronouncements, in the stately cadences of *The Stones of Venice,* that workingmen are at present divided "into mere segments of men," that there is no "right understanding" among classes, and that the great manufacturing centers produce everything save men. In fact, Ruskin concludes, human beings have lost touch with one another in a miasma of commercialism and material acquisition. In the later fifties he pursues these motifs in lecture after lecture and comes to grips ever more firmly with revolutionary social theories that are enunciated in ever clearer and bolder language. Tirelessly, he voices his humane definition of economy as a stewardship and reminds us in one pulsating sentence after another of the sacred obligation implicit in human relationships. He is, in short, sounding the theme of "social affection" inherited from his master Carlyle and supremely expressed in the four articles comprising *Unto this Last.*

By late June, 1860, Ruskin had completed the first essay—and perhaps more—of *Unto This Last,* which he forwarded to his publisher with a letter suggesting insertion in the newly founded *Cornhill Magazine,* then edited by the novelist William Makepeace Thackeray. Ruskin also dispatched a copy to his father, who, although disturbed by what he considered the radicalism of his son's writing, supported him with characteristic loyalty when the critical storms blew hard—and they raged fiercely from the appearance of the initial essay in August, 1860. Most of the journals throughout England and Scotland—invariably supporters of the prevailing economic and social theories—attacked the work as "utter imbecility" and "eruptions of windy hysterics," and excoriated the author as "a perfect paragon of blubbering." As a result, Ruskin was informed that after the third number only one more of his essays would be permitted; he was allowed to extend this in length, but with the appearance in November of "Ad Valorem," the series ended—to the immense relief of both publisher and editor. Not a man to be downed by hostile criticism, Ruskin subsequently added a Preface (printed below) to the four essays and published the whole—again under the title of *Unto this Last*—in 1862. No second edition was called for until 1877, but sales increased by the thousands from that time till the end of the century. Furthermore, Gandhi, Tolstoy, and others deeply concerned with human welfare have, at various times, paid tribute to the enduring values of *Unto this Last*, and Ruskin himself spoke of it as "the only book, properly to be called a book, that I have yet written, the one that will stand (if anything stand) surely and longest of all work of mine."

It is not only the call to humanity, the courageous tilting at entrenched theory, the promulgation of new ideas (many of which have since come to pass), and the brave redefinition of wealth in human terms that makes *Unto this Last* a document of timeless relevance. As a work of art, as a skillfully composed and exquisitely shaped dissertation upon lasting themes, the book stands preeminent, for it is representative of Ruskin's finest writing, which means that it is a landmark in English prose. In paragraph after paragraph one sees how carefully the author has pared away the superfluous, divested passages of anything too colorful or gaudy, and focused his attention solely upon the most expeditious manner of stating his message.

Stylistically *Unto this Last* is a superb example of what can be done with the English language in the hands of a master. In the first place, the fundamental organization of the whole is a salient lesson in sound writing. In the initial essay, for instance, Ruskin smites hard at the opposition in the very first sentence:

> Among the delusions which at different periods have possessed themselves of the minds of large masses of the human race, perhaps the most curious—certainly the least creditable—is the modern *soi-disant* science of political economy, based on the idea that an advantageous code of social action may be determined irrespectively of the influence of social affection.

The controlled length of this sentence, its dignity of utterance, its remarkable balance, its careful employment of subordination, its comprehension of statement, and its massive forward movement, culminating in the focal phrase "social affection," suggest its significance in terms of the whole as the first sounding of a noble theme in, say, a Mahler symphony anticipates the tenor of the music to come.

Then, using the numerous devices at his command, Ruskin moves effortlessly into his argument: the relationship between the workman and the employer. These passages are carefully designed as he explicates, with dazzling expertise, the various qualities and classes of relationship, going deftly from one example to the next, each deriving from a fundamental and easily grasped domestic figure or image.

So subtly does Ruskin work that the reader can easily overlook the devices employed to express his message. In the first essay—meaningfully entitled "The Roots of Honour"—the diction is of primary importance in working to support the basic statement. As Ruskin warms to the subject, the essential words begin to appear: *justice, affection, soul, kindness;* less frequently employed, but still a part of the greater design are, for example, *will, spirit, wholesome,* and *good.* Gradually, by unobtrusive incremental usage, Ruskin's vocabulary, confined to simple words, assumes overtones of enduring significance and creates, as well, an aura of humanity, affection, and controlled sentiment. Such usages are sustained throughout the essays and contribute much to Ruskin's meaning as he moves from one facet of his argument to the next.

Neither should his immense literary heritage be overlooked. The reader is instantly struck by the vast amount of reading that is a background for Ruskin's writing. In *Unto this Last* alone there are allusions to, and derivations from, the Bible, Dante, Shakespeare, Plato, Hesiod, Pope, and many others. He never tires of supporting an argument or sustaining an idea by referring to the literary-philosophical tradition that lies for centuries behind him. In this manner he brings strength, credence, and authority to his statements, as well as muscle and sinew to his prose. Similarly, his metaphors (for example, "the veins of wealth," "the roots of honour") are carefully wrought and, while fundamental to an understanding of a particular aspect of his thought, never overwhelming. Such other

devices as alliteration, consonance, assonance, and
antithesis Ruskin uses, consciously or unconsciously,
with economical discretion in *Unto this Last*; in fact,
one can open the book at random and see how different devices help to clarify what he is saying.[2] Indeed,
the spare, flexible, and lucid quality of Ruskin's prose
in this work demonstrates his writing to better advantage than many of the often quoted luxuriant passages
from *Modern Painters*. In sum, it seems safe to say
that *Unto this Last*, both in form and content, represents literary accomplishment at its highest.

"Traffic," the final essay in this collection, was first
a lecture given by Ruskin in Bradford in 1864; subsequently he published it in a miscellany entitled *The
Crown of Wild Oliver* (1866). While "Traffic" has
much in common with the spirit of *Unto this Last*, it
is designed differently and relies more upon diversifi-
cation than singleness of purpose for its effects. In it
Ruskin, under the guise of giving architectural advice
about the building of a new Exchange, states afresh
some of his familiar ideas about taste as the only morality, the character of a nation residing in its art, the
competition, treachery and jealousy in contemporary
commerce, the sacredness of the earth, and the spirit-

---

[2] Because Ruskin's work—at its finest—is so tightly knit, it is
inadvisable to excerpt from his essays. For that reason *Unto
this Last* and "Traffic" are printed in their entirety—from the
Cook and Wedderburn text in *The Works of John Ruskin* (39
vols., London, 1903-1912), hereafter referred to as *Works*.
Only some of Ruskin's footnotes have been deleted: the text
remains intact. It is unfortunate that most selections from Ruskin are very rarely printed as a whole; omissions within the
individual essays are common. For quick reference the paragraphs in "Traffic" have been renumbered.

uality implicit in good architecture. In contemplating worship, he draws the famous figure of the "Goddess of Getting-on," or as she is also named, "Britannia of the Market." When one ponders the heterogeneities of the essay it becomes clear that another indictment— differently planned from *Unto this Last* yet complementary to it in thought—has been effectively delivered upon the callous rapacity of the age.

What is quite in contrast to *Unto this Last* is the humor of "Traffic." One can wryly imagine the response of the evangelical burghers of Bradford—good *laissez-faire* men all—as Ruskin remarks that he cannot comment on the projected Exchange, continuing with ". . . most simply and sorrowfully, I have to tell you, in the outset, that I do *not* care about this Exchange of yours," or the reaction by the town worthies, assuming their perception to comprehend, to Ruskin's attacks on all they stood for as he draws his vivid picture of the "Goddess of Getting-on." For Ruskin's humour ranged widely from the elegant and graceful (which plays across many a page of his autobiography, *Praeterita*) to an elephantine irony reminiscent of Carlyle. Yet between the two extremes Ruskin often reveals a mordant irony that gives a keen, precise edge to much of his social writings. This spirit moves throughout "Traffic" and is perhaps accountable for its difference in tone from *Unto this Last*. But both works proceed along similar lines and make many identical statements. Both contribute profoundly to our knowledge of Ruskin and to our awareness of the important role a Victorian intellectual—as opposed to his counterpart today in the English-speaking world— could forcefully play. People a century ago listened to Ruskin as they listened to other writers who were courageous enough to present unpopular convictions; and although many opposed what he said and even reviled him personally, those same hostile forces were constantly prodded into thought and into fresh considerations of their positions. If a man could so stimulate his readers—and Ruskin did so increasingly as the century lumbered on—it is clear that he has bequeathed a valuable legacy to the human condition.

PRINCIPAL DATES
IN THE LIFE OF RUSKIN

1819 Born, the son of Margaret and John James Ruskin, at 54 Hunter Street, London.

1825 Makes first Continental tour. For the rest of his life this is to be an almost annual events.

1826 Commences writing verse.

1830 Tours the Lake District. Makes first apance in print—in the *Spiritual Times*—with a poem "On Skiddaw and Derwent Water."

1831 Takes drawing lessons.

1832 Receives Christmas present of Rogers' *Italy*, which initiates his interest in the painter, Turner.

1834 First prose publication appears in Loudon's *Magazine of Natural History*.

1835 Sees Venice for the first time.

1836 Writes (but does not publish) a reply to *Blackwood's* attack on Turner; later comments that his defense of the artist was the genesis of *Modern Painters*. Matriculates at Christ Church, Oxford, in October.

1837-8 Publishes "The Poetry of Architecture" in the *Architectural Magazine*.

1840 Leaves Oxford without a degree because of illness: the first of numerous physical or mental disturbances.

1842   Relinquishes idea of taking Holy Orders. Receives Oxford degree.

1843   Publishes *Modern Painters I*.

1845   Reads Sismondi; stirrings of social awareness develop.

1846   Publishes *Modern Painters II*.

1848   Marries Euphemia Chalmers Gray.

1849   Publishes *The Seven Lamps of Architecture*.

1849-50   In Venice, working on *The Stones of Venice*.

1851   Publishes *The Stones of Venice I*. Defends Pre-Raphaelite movement. Returns to Venice to work on *Stones*.

1853   Publishes *The Stones of Venice II, III*. Takes Scottish holiday with wife and the painter, Millais.

1854   Marriage annulled, his wife marrying Millais the following year. Growing friendship with Dante Gabriel Rossetti and Elizabeth Siddal. Commences close association with the Working Men's College.

1856   Publishes *Modern Painters III, IV*.

1857-59   Years of varied activity writing, lecturing, cataloguing, sketching, and traveling. Experiences (1858) a revision of his evangelical views and subscribes to a "religion of humanity."

1860   Fifth and final volume of *Modern Painters* published. The four essays comprising *Unto this Last* (1862) first appear in the *Cornhill Magazine* (August-November).

1862-63   "Essays on Political Economy" appear in *Fraser's Magazine*. With much revision they are later published in book form as *Munera Pulveris* (1872).

1864   Death of his father, John James Ruskin, from whom he inherits a great deal of money.

1865   Publishes *Sesame and Lilies*.

1866   Publishes *The Ethics of the Dust* and *The Crown of Wild Olive*, of which "Traffic" (originally given in 1864) is the second lecture. The years 1866-1875 are times of terrible emotional stress because of his blighted love for the young Irish girl, Rose La Touche. She is to recur symbolically through his work for the years to come. Ruskin's own interests are to become increasingly diffuse as the decades pass.

1867   Publishes *Time and Tide, by Weare and Tyne*, a series of letters given to social problems.

1869   Publishes *The Queen of the Air* (on myth)

1870   In February he gives the inaugural lecture at Oxford as Slade Professor of Fine Art.

1871   Commences the epistolary *Fors Clavigera*, which runs, with some interruptions, until the mid eighties. Very seriously ill at Matlock during the summer. Purchases "Brantwood" in the Lake District where he is to spend most of his remaining years. Manifests deepening interest in the St. George's Fund and embarks upon various schemes for social amelioration such as street-cleaning and road-digging. His mother dies aged ninety.

1872   Publishes two series of Oxford lectures:

Aratra Pentilici (on sculpture) and *The Eagle's Nest* (on science and art).

1873   Commences ornithological lectures at Oxford to be published as *Love's Meinie* (1873-1881).

1874   Publishes *Val d'Arno*, Oxford lectures on Tuscan art. His religious attitudes are modified—this time toward a "more definitely Christian" form of belief.

1875   Death of Rose La Touche. His publications and lectures continue to proliferate. Dabbles in spiritualism.

1876   Publishes another series of collected Oxford lectures, *Ariadne Florentina*, dealing with wood and metal engraving.

1877   Sixth and final part of *Mornings in Florence* published; preceding parts appeared in 1875-76. Attack on Whistler in *Fors* (Letter 79) evokes a libel suit in which Ruskin—too ill to appear—is fined damages of one farthing.

1878   Suffers an extremely severe mental attack, the first of several to occur during the next decade. Is constituted first master of St. George's Guild.

1879   Resigns Oxford professorship.

1880-81 Publishes "Fiction Fair and Foul," some of his most provocative and rewarding literary criticism. Commences (1880) publication of *The Bible of Amiens*, distinguished as one of his finest late works.

1883   Resumption of Oxford professorship, which terminates under unfortunate circumstances in 1885.

1885   Commences the publication, in parts, of his autobiography, *Praeterita*, one of his most exquisite and sustained prose writings.

1889-1900   Suffers an incapacitating mental attack in the summer of 1889 and, until his death on 20 January 1900, is almost wholly an invalid at "Brantwood."

UNTO THIS LAST

and

TRAFFIC

UNTO THIS LAST

Preface

1. The four following essays were published eighteen months ago in the *Cornhill Magazine,* and were reprobated in a violent manner, as far as I could hear, by most of the readers they met with.

Not a whit the less, I believe them to be the best, that is to say, the truest, rightest-worded, and most serviceable things I have ever written; and the last of them, having had especial pains spent on it, is probably the best I shall ever write.

"This," the reader may reply, "it might be, yet not therefore well written." Which, in no mock humility, admitting, I yet rest satisfied with the work, though with nothing else that I have done; and purposing shortly to follow out the subjects opened in these papers, as I may find leisure,[1] I wish the introductory statements to be within the reach of any one who may care to refer to them. So I republish the essays as they appeared. One word only is changed, correcting the estimate of a weight; and no word is added.

2. Although, however, I find nothing to modify in these papers, it is a matter of regret to me that the most startling of all the statements in them,—that respecting the necessity of the organization of labour,

[1] As he did, for example, in *Munera Pulveris.*

1

with fixed wages,—should have found its way into the first essay; it being quite one of the least important, though by no means the least certain, of the positions to be defended. The real gist of these papers, their central meaning and aim, is to give, as I believe for the first time in plain English,—it has often been incidentally given in good Greek by Plato and Xenophon, and good Latin by Cicero and Horace,—a logical definition of WEALTH: such definition being absolutely needed for a basis of economical science. The most reputed essay on that subject which has appeared in modern times, after opening with the statement that "writers on political economy profess to teach, or to investigate, the nature of wealth," thus follows up the declaration of its thesis—"Every one has a notion, sufficiently correct for common purposes, of what is meant by wealth.". . . "It is no part of the design of this treatise to aim at metaphysical nicety of definition." [2]

3. Metaphysical nicety, we assuredly do not need; but physical nicety, and logical accuracy, with respect to a physical subject, we as assuredly do.

Suppose the subject of inquiry, instead of being House-law (*Oikonomia*), had been Star-law (*Astronomia*), and that, ignoring distinction between stars fixed and wandering, as here between wealth radiant and wealth reflective, the writer had begun thus: "Every one has a notion, sufficiently correct for common purposes, of what is meant by stars. Metaphysical nicety in the definition of a star is not the object of this treatise";—the essay so opened might yet have been far more true in its final statements, and a thousandfold more serviceable to the navigator, than any

[2] From the *Principles of Political Economy* by John Stuart Mill.

treatise on wealth, which founds its conclusions on the popular conception of wealth, can ever become to the economist.

4. It was, therefore, the first object of these following papers to give an accurate and stable definition of wealth. Their second object was to show that the acquisition of wealth was finally possible only under certain moral conditions of society, of which quite the first was a belief in the existence, and even, for practical purposes, in the attainability of honesty.

Without venturing to pronounce—since on such a matter human judgment is by no means conclusive—what is, or is not, the noblest of God's works, we may yet admit so much of Pope's assertion as that an honest man is among His best works presently visible,[3] and, as things stand, a somewhat rare one; but not an incredible or miraculous work; still less an abnormal one. Honesty is not a disturbing force, which deranges the orbits of economy; but a consistent and commanding force, by obedience to which—and by no other obedience—those orbits can continue clear of chaos.

5. It is true, I have sometimes heard Pope condemned for the lowness, instead of the height, of his standard:—"Honesty is indeed a respectable virtue; but how much higher may men attain! Shall nothing more be asked of us than that we be honest?"

For the present, good friends, nothing. It seems that in our aspirations to be more than that, we have to some extent lost sight of the propriety of being so much as that. What else we may have lost faith in, there shall be here no question; but assuredly we have lost faith in common honesty, and in the working power of it. And this faith, with the facts on which it

[3] *An Essay on Man,* Epistle iv, 1. 248.

may rest, it is quite our first business to recover and
keep: not only believing, but even by experience as-
suring ourselves, that there are yet in the world men
who can be restrained from fraud otherwise than by
the fear of losing employment; nay, that it is even accurately in proportion to the number of such men in
any State, that the said State does or can prolong its
existence.

To these two points, then, the following essays are
mainly directed. The subject of the organization of labour is only casually touched upon; because, if we
once can get a sufficient quantity of honesty in our
captains,[4] the organization of labour is easy, and will
develop itself without quarrel or difficulty; but if we
cannot get honesty in our captains, the organization
of labour is for evermore impossible.

6. The several conditions of its possibility I purpose
to examine at length in the sequel. Yet, lest the reader
should be alarmed by the hints thrown out during the
following investigation of first principles, as if they
were leading him into unexpectedly dangerous ground,
I will, for his better assurance, state at once the worst
of the political creed at which I wish him to arrive.

(1.) First,—that there should be training schools
for youth established, at Government cost, and under
Government discipline, over the whole country; that
every child born in the country should, at the parent's
wish, be permitted (and, in certain cases, be under
penalty required) to pass through them; and that, in
these schools, the child should (with other minor
pieces of knowledge hereafter to be considered) imperatively be taught, with the best skill of teaching
that the country could produce, the following three

[4] Of industry.

things:—(*a*) The laws of health, and the exercises enjoined by them; (*b*) Habits of gentleness and justice; and (*c*) The calling by which he is to live.

(2.) Secondly,—that, in connection with these training schools, there should be established, and also entirely under Government regulation, manufactories and workshops for the production and sale of every necessary of life, and for the exercise of every useful art. And that, interfering no whit with private enterprise, nor setting any restraints or tax on private trade, but leaving both to do their best, and beat the Government if they could,—there should, at these Government manufactories and shops, be authoritatively good and exemplary work done, and pure and true substance sold; so that a man could be sure, if he chose to pay the Government price, that he got for his money bread that was bread, ale that was ale, and work that was work.[5]

(3.) Thirdly,—that any man, or woman, or boy, or girl, out of employment, should be at once received at the nearest Government school, and set to such work as it appeared, on trial, they were fit for, at a fixed rate of wages determinable every year;—that, being found incapable of work through ignorance, they should be taught, or being found incapable of work through sickness, should be tended; but that being found objecting to work, they should be set, under compulsion of the strictest nature, to the more painful and degrading forms of necessary toil, especially to

[5] Ruskin is here tilting at Adam Smith's statement in *The Wealth of Nations* (Book I, ch. x) that "The real and effectual discipline which is exercised over a workman, is not that of his corporation, but of his customers. It is the fear of losing their employment which restrains his frauds and corrects his negligence."

that in mines and other places of danger (such danger being, however, diminished to the utmost by careful regulation and discipline), and the due wages of such work be retained, cost of compulsion first abstracted— to be at the workman's command, so soon as he has come to sounder mind respecting the laws of employment.

(4.) Lastly,—that for the old and destitute, comfort and home should be provided; which provision, when misfortune had been by the working of such a system sifted from guilt, would be honourable instead of disgraceful to the receiver. For (I repeat this passage out of my *Political Economy of Art,* to which the reader is referred for farther detail) "a labourer serves his country with his spade, just as a man in the middle ranks of life serves it with sword, pen, or lancet. If the service be less, and, therefore, the wages during health less, then the reward when health is broken may be less, but not less honourable; and it ought to be quite as natural and straightforward a matter for a labourer to take his pension from his parish, because he has deserved well of his parish, as for a man in higher rank to take his pension from his country, because he has deserved well of his country."

To which statement, I will only add for conclusion, respecting the discipline and pay of life and death, that, for both high and low, Livy's last words touching Valerius Publicola, *"de publico est elatus,"* [6] ought not be a dishonourable close of epitaph.

7. These things, then, I believe, and am about, as I find power, to explain and illustrate in their various

---

[6] For "elatus" read "datus." Translated, the phrase means that Publius Valerius was buried at the expense of the public treasury.

bearings; following out also what belongs to them of collateral inquiry. Here I state them only in brief, to prevent the reader casting about in alarm for my ultimate meaning; yet requesting him, for the present, to remember, that in a science dealing with so subtle elements as those of human nature, it is only possible to answer for the final truth of principles, not for the direct success of plans: and that in the best of these last, what can be immediately accomplished is always questionable, and what can be finally accomplished, inconceivable.

Denmark Hill,
    10*th May,* 1862.

UNTO THIS LAST

Essay I

THE ROOTS OF HONOUR

1. Among the delusions which at different periods have possessed themselves of the minds of large masses of the human race, perhaps the most curious— certainly the least creditable—is the modern *soi-disant* science of political economy, based on the idea that an advantageous code of social action may be determined irrespectively of the influence of social affection.

Of course, as in the instances of alchemy, astrology, witchcraft, and other such popular creeds, political economy has a plausible idea at the root of it. "The social affections," says the economist, "are accidental and disturbing elements in human nature; but avarice and the desire of progress are constant elements. Let us eliminate the inconstants, and, considering the human being merely as a covetous machine, examine by what laws of labour, purchase, and sale, the greatest accumulative result in wealth is obtainable. Those laws once determined, it will be for each individual afterwards to introduce as much of the disturbing affectionate element as he chooses, and to determine for himself the result on the new conditions supposed."

2. This would be a perfectly logical and successful

method of analysis, if the accidentals afterwards to be introduced were of the same nature as the powers first examined. Supposing a body in motion to be influenced by constant and inconstant forces, it is usually the simplest way of examining its course to trace it first under the persistent conditions, and afterwards introduce the causes of variation. But the disturbing elements in the social problem are not of the same nature as the constant ones: they alter the essence of the creature under examination the moment they are added; they operate, not mathematically, but chemically, introducing conditions which render all our previous knowledge unavailable. We made learned experiments upon pure nitrogen, and have convinced ourselves that it is a very manageable gas: but, behold! the thing which we have practically to deal with is its chloride; and this, the moment we touch it on our established principles, sends us and our apparatus through the ceiling.

3. Observe, I neither impugn nor doubt the conclusion of the science if its terms are accepted. I am simply uninterested in them, as I should be in those of a science of gymnastics which assumed that men had no skeletons. It might be shown, on that supposition, that it would be advantageous to roll the students up into pellets, flatten them into cakes, or stretch them into cables; and that when these results were effected, the re-insertion of the skeleton would be attended with various inconveniences to their constitution. The reasoning might be admirable, the conclusions true, and the science deficient only in applicability. Modern political economy stands on a precisely similar basis. Assuming, not that the human being has no skeleton, but that it is all skeleton, it

founds an ossifiant theory of progress on this negation
of a soul; and having shown the utmost that may be
made of bones, and constructed a number of interesting geometrical figures with death's-head and humeri,
successfully proves the inconvenience of the reappear-
ance of a soul among these corpuscular structures. I
do not deny the truth of this theory: I simply deny
its applicability to the present phase of the world.

4. This inapplicability has been curiously mani-
fested during the embarrassment caused by the late
strikes of our workmen. Here occurs one of the simplest cases, in a pertinent and positive form, of the
first vital problem which political economy has to deal
with (the relation between employer and employed);
and, at a severe crisis, when lives in multitudes and
wealth in masses are at stake, the political economists
are helpless—practically mute: no demonstrable so-
lution of the difficulty can be given by them, such as
may convince or calm the opposing parties. Obsti-
nately the masters take one view of the matter; obsti-
nately the operatives another; and no political science
can set them at one.

5. It would be strange if it could, it being not by
"science" of any kind that men were ever intended
to be set at one. Disputant after disputant vainly
strives to show that the interests of the masters are,
or are not, antagonistic to those of the men: none of
the pleaders ever seeming to remember that it does not
absolutely or always follow that the persons must be
antagonistic because their interests are. If there is only
a crust of bread in the house, and mother and children
are starving, their interests are not the same. If the
mother eats it, the children want it; if the children
eat it, the mother must go hungry to her work. Yet it

does not necessarily follow that there will be "antagonism" between them, that they will fight for the crust, and that the mother, being strongest, will get it, and eat it. Neither, in any other case, whatever the relations of the persons may be, can it be assumed for certain that, because their interests are diverse, they must necessarily regard each other with hostility, and use violence or cunning to obtain the advantage.

6. Even if this were so, and it were as just as it is convenient to consider men as actuated by no other moral influences than those which affect rats or swine, the logical conditions of the question are still indeterminable. It can never be shown generally either that the interests of master and labourer are alike, or that they are opposed; for, according to circumstances, they may be either. It is, indeed, always the interest of both that the work should be rightly done, and a just price obtained for it; but, in the division of profits, the gain of the one may or may not be the loss of the other. It is not the master's interest to pay wages so low as to leave the men sickly and depressed, nor the workman's interest to be paid high wages if the smallness of the master's profit hinders him from enlarging his business, or conducting it in a safe and liberal way. A stoker ought not to desire high pay if the company is too poor to keep the engine-wheels in repair.

7. And the varieties of circumstance which influence these reciprocal interests are so endless, that all endeavour to deduce rules of action from balance of expediency is in vain. And it is meant to be in vain. For no human actions ever were intended by the Maker of men to be guided by balances of expediency, but by balances of justice. He has therefore rendered all endeavours to determine expediency futile for

evermore. No man ever knew, or can know, what will be the ultimate result to himself, or to others, of any given line of conduct. But every man may know, and most of us do know, what is a just and unjust act. And all of us may know also, that the consequences of justice will be ultimately the best possible, both to others and ourselves, though we can neither say what *is* best, or how it is likely to come to pass.

I have said balances of justice, meaning, in the term justice, to include affection,—such affection as one man *owes* to another. All right relations between master and operative, and all their best interests, ultimately depend on these.

8. We shall find the best and simplest illustration of the relations of master and operative in the position of domestic servants.

We will suppose that the master of a household desires only to get as much work out of his servants as he can, at the rate of wages he gives. He never allows them to be idle; feeds them as poorly and lodges them as ill as they will endure, and in all things pushes his requirements to the exact point beyond which he cannot go without forcing the servant to leave him. In doing this, there is no violation on his part of what is commonly called "justice." He agrees with the domestic for his whole time and service, and takes them; —the limits of hardship in treatment being fixed by the practice of other masters in his neighbourhood; that is to say, by the current rate of wages for domestic labour. If the servant can get a better place, he is free to take one, and the master can only tell what is the real market value of his labour, by requiring as much as he will give.

This is the politico-economical view of the case, according to the doctors of that science; who assert that by this procedure the greatest average of work will be obtained from the servant, and therefore the greatest benefit to the community, and through the community, by reversion, to the servant himself.

That, however, is not so. It would be so if the servant were an engine of which the motive power was steam, magnetism, gravitation, or any other agent of calculable force. But he being, on the contrary, an engine whose motive power is a Soul, the force of this very peculiar agent, as an unknown quantity, enters into all the political economist's equations, without his knowledge, and falsifies every one of their results. The largest quantity of work will not be done by this curious engine for pay, or under pressure, or by help of any kind of fuel which may be supplied by the chaldron. It will be done only when the motive force, that is to say, the will or spirit of the creature, is brought to its greatest strength by its own proper fuel: namely, by the affections.

9. It may indeed happen, and does happen often, that if the master is a man of sense and energy, a large quantity of material work may be done under mechanical pressure, enforced by strong will and guided by wise method; also it may happen, and does happen often, that if the master is indolent and weak (however good-natured), a very small quantity of work, and that bad, may be produced by the servant's undirected strength, and contemptuous gratitude. But the universal law of the matter is that, assuming any given quantity of energy and sense in master and servant, the greatest material result obtainable by them will be, not through antagonism to each other, but through affection for each other; and that, if the

master, instead of endeavouring to get as much work as possible from the servant, seeks rather to render his appointed and necessary work beneficial to him, and to forward his interests in all just and wholesome ways, the real amount of work ultimately done, or of good rendered, by the person so cared for, will indeed be the greatest possible.

Observe, I say, "of good rendered," for a servant's work is not necessarily or always the best thing he can give his master. But good of all kinds, whether in material service, in protective watchfulness of his master's interest and credit, or in joyful readiness to seize unexpected and irregular occasions of help.

Nor is this one whit less generally true because indulgence will be frequently abused, and kindness met with ingratitude. For the servant who, gently treated, is ungrateful, treated ungently, will be revengeful; and the man who is dishonest to a liberal master will be injurious to an unjust one.

10. In any case, and with any person, this unselfish treatment will produce the most effective return. Observe, I am here considering the affections wholly as a motive power; not at all as things in themselves desirable or noble, or in any other way abstractedly good. I look at them simply as an anomalous force, rendering every one of the ordinary political economist's calculations nugatory; while, even if he desired to introduce this new element into his estimates, he has no power of dealing with it; for the affections only become a true motive power when they ignore every other motive and condition of political economy. Treat the servant kindly, with the idea of turning his gratitude to account, and you will get, as you deserve, no gratitude, nor any value for your kindness; but treat

him kindly without any economical purpose, and all
economical purposes will be answered; in this, as in
all other matters, whosoever will save his life shall
lose it, whoso loses it shall find it.[1]

11. The next clearest and simplest example of relation between master and operative is that which

---

[1] Cf. Matthew 16:25. Ruskin appends to this paragraph a long
and interesting note revealing of his powers of literary analysis.
It runs as follows:

The difference between the two modes of treatment, and
between their effective material results may be seen very
accurately by a comparison of the relations of Esther and
Charlie in *Bleak House* with those of Miss Brass and the
Marchioness in *Master Humphrey's Clock*.

The essential value and truth of Dickens's writings have
been unwisely lost sight of by many thoughtful persons,
merely because he presents his truth with some colour of
caricature. Unwisely, because Dickens's caricature, though
often gross, is never mistaken. Allowing for his manner of
telling them, the things he tells us are always true. I wish
that he could think it right to limit his brilliant exaggeration
to works written only for public amusement; and when he
takes up a subject of high national importance, such as that
which he handled in *Hard Times*, that he would use severer
and more accurate analysis. The usefulness of that work
(to my mind, in several respects the greatest he has written)
is with many persons seriously diminished because Mr.
Bounderby is a dramatic monster, instead of a characteristic
example of a worldly master; and Stephen Blackpool a
dramatic perfection, instead of a characteristic example of
an honest workman. But let us not lose the use of Dickens's
wit and insight, because he chooses to speak in a circle of
stage fire. He is entirely right in his main drift and purpose
in every book he has written; and all of them, but especially
Hard Times, should be studied with close and earnest care
by persons interested in social questions. They will find much
that is partial, and, because partial, apparently unjust; but if
they examine all the evidence on the other side, which
Dickens seems to overlook, it will appear, after all their
trouble, that his view was the finally right one, grossly and
sharply told.

exists between the commander of a regiment and his men.

Supposing the officer only desires to apply the rules of discipline so as, with least trouble to himself, to make the regiment most effective, he will not be able, by any rules or administration of rules, on this selfish principle, to develop the full strength of his subordinates. If a man of sense and firmness, he may, as in the former instance, produce a better result than would be obtained by the irregular kindness of a weak officer; but let the sense and firmness be the same in both cases, and assuredly the officer who has the most direct personal relations with his men, the most care for their interests, and the most value for their lives, will develop their effective strength, through their affection for his own person, and trust in his character, to a degree wholly unattainable by other means. This law applies still more stringently as the numbers concerned are larger: a charge may often be successful, though the men dislike their officers; a battle has rarely been won, unless they loved their general.

12. Passing from these simple examples to the more complicated relations existing between a manufacturer and his workmen, we are met first by certain curious difficulties, resulting, apparently, from a harder and colder state of moral elements. It is easy to imagine an enthusiastic affection existing among soldiers for the colonel. Not so easy to imagine an enthusiastic affection among cotton-spinners for the proprietor of the mill. A body of men associated for purposes of robbery (as a Highland clan in ancient times) shall be animated by perfect affection, and every member of it be ready to lay down his life for the life of his chief. But a band of men associated for purposes of

legal production and accumulation is usually animated, it appears, by no such emotions, and none of
them are [*sic.*] in any wise willing to give his life for the
life of his chief. Not only are we met by this apparent
anomaly, in moral matters, but by others connected
with it, in administration of system. For a servant or
a soldier is engaged at a definite rate of wages, for a
definite period; but a workman at a rate of wages
variable according to the demand for labour, and with
the risk of being at any time thrown out of his situ-
ation by chances of trade. Now, as, under these
contingencies, no action of the affections can take
place, but only an explosive action of *dis*affections,
two points offer themselves for consideration in the
matter.

The first—How far the rate of wages may be so
regulated as not to vary with the demand for labour.

The second—How far it is possible that bodies of
workmen may be engaged and maintained at such
fixed rate of wages (whatever the state of trade may
be), without enlarging or diminishing their number,
so as to give them permanent interest in the establishment with which they are connected, like that of
the domestic servants in an old family, or an *esprit de
corps*, like that of the soldiers in a crack regiment.

13. The first question is, I say, how far it may be
possible to fix the rate of wages, irrespectively of the
demand for labour.

Perhaps one of the most curious facts in the history
of human error is the denial by the common political
economist of the possibility of thus regulating wages;
while, for all the important, and much of the unim-
portant, labour, on the earth, wages are already so
regulated.

We do not sell our prime-ministership by Dutch auction; nor, on the decease of a bishop, whatever may be the general advantages of simony, do we (yet) offer his diocese to the clergyman who will take the episcopacy at the lowest contract. We (with exquisite sagacity of political economy!) do indeed sell commissions; but not openly, generalships: sick, we do not inquire for a physician who takes less than a guinea; litigious, we never think of reducing six-and-eightpence to four-and-sixpence; caught in a shower, we do not canvass the cabmen, to find one who values his driving at less than sixpence a mile.

It is true that in all these cases there is, and in every conceivable case there must be, ultimate reference to the presumed difficulty of the work, or number of candidates for the office. If it were thought that the labour necessary to make a good physician would be gone through by a sufficient number of students with the prospect of only half-guinea fees, public consent would soon withdraw the unnecessary half-guinea. In this ultimate sense, the price of labour is indeed always regulated by the demand for it; but, so far as the practical and immediate administration of the matter is regarded, the best labour always has been, and is, as *all* labour ought to be, paid by an invariable standard.

14. "What!" the reader perhaps answers amazedly: "pay good and bad workmen alike?"

Certainly. The difference between one prelate's sermons and his successor's—or between one physician's opinion and another's,—is far greater, as respects the qualities of mind involved, and far more important in result to you personally, than the difference between good and bad laying of bricks (though that is greater than most people suppose). Yet you pay with equal fee, contentedly, the good and bad workmen upon your soul, and the good and bad workmen upon your body; much more may you pay, contentedly, with equal fees, the good and bad workmen upon your house.

"Nay, but I choose my physician, and (?) my clergyman, thus indicating my sense of the quality of their work." By all means, also, choose your bricklayer; that is the proper reward of the good workman, to be "chosen." The natural and right system respecting all labour is, that it should be paid at a fixed rate, but the good workman employed, and the bad workman unemployed. The false, unnatural, and destructive system is when the bad workman is allowed to offer his work at half-price, and either take the place of the good, or force him by his competition to work for an inadequate sum.

15. This equality of wages, then, being the first object towards which we have to discover the directest available road, the second is, as above stated, that of maintaining constant numbers of workmen in employment, whatever may be the accidental demand for the article they produce.

I believe the sudden and extensive inequalities of demand, which necessarily arise in the mercantile operations of an active nation, constitute the only essential difficulty which has to be overcome in a just organization of labour.

The subject opens into too many branches to admit of being investigated in a paper of this kind; but the following general facts bearing on it may be noted.

The wages which enable any workman to live are necessarily higher, if his work is liable to intermission, than if it is assured and continuous; and however severe the struggle for work may become, the general law will always hold, that men must get more daily pay if, on the average, they can only calculate on work three days a week than they would require if they were sure of work six days a week. Supposing that a man cannot live on less than a shilling a day, his seven shillings he must get, either for three days' violent work, or six days' deliberate work. The tendency of all modern mercantile operations is to throw both wages and trade into the form of a lottery, and to make the workman's pay depend on intermittent exertion, and the principal's profit on dexterously used chance.

16. In what partial degree, I repeat, this may be necessary in consequence of the activities of modern trade, I do not here investigate; contenting myself with the fact that in its fatallest aspects it is assuredly unnecessary, and results merely from love of gambling on the part of the masters, and from ignorance and sensuality in the men. The masters cannot bear to let any opportunity of gain escape them, and frantically rush at every gap and breach in the walls of Fortune, raging to be rich, and affronting, with impatient covetousness, every risk of ruin, while the men prefer three days of violent labour, and three days of drunkenness, to six days of moderate work and wise rest. There is no way in which a principal, who really desires to help his workmen, may do it more effectually than by checking these disorderly habits both in himself and them; keeping his own business operations on a scale which will enable him to pursue them securely, not yielding to temptations of precarious gain; and at the same time, leading his workmen into regular

habits of labour and life, either by inducing them rather to take low wages, in the form of a fixed salary, than high wages, subject to the chance of their being thrown out of work; or, if this be impossible, by discouraging the system of violent exertion for nominally high day wages, and leading the men to take lower pay for more regular labour.

In effecting any radical changes of this kind, doubtless there would be great inconvenience and loss incurred by all the originators of the movement. That which can be done with perfect convenience and without loss, is not always the thing that most needs to be done, or which we are most imperatively required to do.

17. I have already alluded to the difference hitherto existing between regiments of men associated for purposes of violence, and for purposes of manufacture; in that the former appear capable of self-sacrifice—the latter, not; which singular fact is the real reason of the general lowness of estimate in which the profession of commerce is held, as compared with that of arms. Philosophically, it does not, at first sight, appear reasonable (many writers have endeavoured to prove it unreasonable) that a peaceable and rational person, whose trade is buying and selling, should be held in less honour than an unpeaceable and often irrational person, whose trade is slaying. Nevertheless, the consent of mankind has always, in spite of the philosophers, given precedence to the soldier.

And this is right.

For the soldier's trade, verily and essentially, is not slaying, but being slain. This, without well knowing its own meaning, the world honours it for. A bravo's trade is slaying; but the world has never respected bravos more than merchants; the reason it honours the soldier is, because he holds his life at the service of the State. Reckless he may be—fond of pleasure or of adventure—all kinds of bye-motives and mean impulses may have determined the choice of his profession, and may affect (to all appearance exclusively) his daily conduct in it; but our estimate of him is based on this ultimate fact—of which we are well assured—that put him in a fortress breach, with all the pleasures of the world behind him, and only death and his duty in front of him, he will keep his face to the front; and he knows that his choice may be put to him at any moment—and has before-hand taken his part—virtually takes such part con-tinually—does, in reality, die daily.[2]

18. Not less is the respect we pay to the lawyer and physician, founded ultimately on their self-sac-rifice. Whatever the learning or acuteness of a great lawyer, our chief respect for him depends on our belief that, set in a judge's seat, he will strive to judge justly, come of it what may. Could we suppose that he would take bribes, and use his acuteness and legal knowledge to give plausibility to iniquitous de-cisions, no degree of intellect would win for him our respect. Nothing will win it, short of our tacit con-viction, that in all important acts of his life justice is first with him; his own interest, second.

In the case of a physician, the ground of the honour we render him is clearer still. Whatever his science, we would shrink from him in horror if we found him regard his patients merely as subjects to experi-ment upon; much more, if we found that, receiving bribes from persons interested in their deaths, he was

[2] I Corinthians 15:31.

using his best skill to give poison in the mask of medicine.

Finally, the principle holds with utmost clearness as it respects clergymen. No goodness of disposition will excuse want of science in a physician, or of shrewdness in an advocate; but a clergyman, even though his power of intellect be small, is respected on the presumed ground of his unselfishness and serviceableness.

19. Now, there can be no question but that the tact, foresight, decision, and other mental powers, required for the successful management of a large mercantile concern, if not such as could be compared with those of a great lawyer, general, or divine, would at least match the general conditions of mind required in the subordinate officers of a ship, or of a regiment, or in the curate of a country parish. If, therefore, all the efficient members of the so-called liberal professions are still, somehow, in public estimate of honour, preferred before the head of a commercial firm, the reason must lie deeper in the measurement of their several powers of mind.

And the essential reason for such preference will be found to lie in the fact that the merchant is presumed to act always selfishly. His work may be very necessary to the community; but the motive of it is understood to be wholly personal. The merchant's first object in all his dealings must be (the public believe) to get as much for himself, and leave as little to his neighbour (or customer) as possible. Enforcing this upon him, by political statute, as the necessary principle of his action; recommending it to him on all occasions, and themselves reciprocally adopting it, proclaiming vociferously, for law of the universe, that a buyer's function is to cheapen, and a seller's to cheat,—the public, nevertheless, involuntarily condemn the man of commerce for his compliance with their own statement, and stamp him for ever as belonging to an inferior grade of human personality.

20. This they will find, eventually, they must give up doing. They must not cease to condemn selfishness; but they will have to discover a kind of commerce which is not exclusively selfish. Or, rather, they will have to discover that there never was, or can be, any other kind of commerce; that this which they have called commerce was not commerce at all, but cozening; and that a true merchant differs as much from a merchant according to laws of modern political economy, as the hero of the *Excursion*[3] from Autolycus.[4] They will find that commerce is an occupation which gentlemen will every day see more need to engage in, rather than in the business of talking to men, or slaying them; that, in true commerce, as in true preaching, or true fighting, it is necessary to admit the idea of occasional voluntary loss;—that sixpences have to be lost, as well as lives, under a sense of duty; that the market may have its martyrdoms as well as the pulpit; and trade its heroisms as well as war.

May have—in the final issue, must have—and only has not had yet, because men of heroic temper have always been misguided in their youth into other fields; not recognizing what is in our days, perhaps, the most important of all fields; so that, while many a zealous person loses his life in trying to teach the form of a gospel, very few will lose a hundred pounds in showing the practice of one.

[3] By William Wordsworth.
[4] Cf. *The Winter's Tale.*

21. The fact is, that people never have had clearly explained to them the true functions of a merchant with respect to other people. I should like the reader to be very clear about this.

Five great intellectual professions, relating to daily necessities of life, have hitherto existed—three exist necessarily, in every civilized nation:

> The Soldier's profession is to *defend* it.
> The Pastor's to *teach* it.
> The Physician's to *keep it in health*.
> The Lawyer's to *enforce justice* in it.
> The Merchant's to *provide* for it.

And the duty of all these men is, on due occasion, to *die* for it.

"On due occasion," namely:—

> The Soldier, rather than leave his post in battle.
> The Physician, rather than leave his post in plague.
> The Pastor, rather than teach Falsehood.
> The Lawyer, rather than countenance Injustice.
> The Merchant—what is *his* "due occasion" of death?

22. It is the main question for the merchant, as for all of us. For, truly, the man who does not know when to die, does not know how to live.

Observe, the merchant's function (or manufacturer's, for in the broad sense in which it is here used the word must be understood to include both) is to provide for the nation. It is no more his function to get profit for himself out of that provision than it is a clergyman's function to get his stipend. This stipend is a due and necessary adjunct, but not the object of his life, if he be a true clergyman, any more than his fee (or honorarium) is the object of life to a true physician. Neither is his fee the object of life to a true merchant. All three, if true men, have a work to be done irrespective of fee—to be done even at any cost, or for quite the contrary of fee; the pastor's function being to teach, the physician's to heal, and the merchant's, as I have said, to provide. That is to say, he has to understand to their very root the qualities of the thing he deals in, and the means of obtaining or producing it; and he has to apply all his sagacity and energy to the producing or obtaining it in perfect state, and distributing it at the cheapest possible price where it is most needed.

And because the production or obtaining of any commodity involves necessarily the agency of many lives and hands, the merchant becomes in the course of his business the master and governor of large masses of men in a more direct, though less confessed way, than a military officer or pastor; so that on him falls, in great part, the responsibility for the kind of life they lead: and it becomes his duty, not only to be always considering how to produce what he sells, in the purest and cheapest forms, but how to make the various employments involved in the production, or transference of it, most beneficial to the men employed.

23. And as into these two functions, requiring for their right exercise the highest intelligence, as well as patience, kindness, and tact, the merchant is bound to put all his energy, so for their just discharge he is bound, as soldier or physician is bound, to give up, if need be, his life, in such way as it may be demanded of him. Two main points he has in his providing function to maintain: first, his engagements (faithful-

ness to engagements being the real root of all pos-
sibilities, in commerce); and, secondly, the perfectness
and purity of the thing provided; so that, rather than
fail in any engagement, or consent to any deterioration,
adulteration, or unjust and exorbitant price of that
which he provides, he is bound to meet fearlessly any
form of distress, poverty, or labour, which may,
through maintenance of these points, come upon him.

24. Again: in his office as governor of the men
employed by him, the merchant or manufacturer is
invested with a distinctly paternal authority and
responsibility. In most cases, a youth entering a
commercial establishment is withdrawn altogether
from home influence; his master must become his
father. else he has, for practical and constant help,
no father at hand: in all cases the master's authority,
together with the general tone and atmosphere of
his business, and the character of the men with whom
the youth is compelled in the course of it to associate,
have more immediate and pressing weight than the
home influence, and will usually neutralize it either
for good or evil; so that the only means which the
master has of doing justice to the men employed by
him is to ask himself sternly whether he is dealing
with such subordinate as he would with his own son,
if compelled by circumstances to take such a position.

Supposing the captain of a frigate saw it right, or
were by any chance obliged, to place his own son in
the position of a common sailor: as he would then
treat his son, he is bound always to treat every one
of the men under him. So, also, supposing the master
of a manufactory saw it right, or were by any chance
obliged, to place his own son in the position of an
ordinary workman; as he would then treat his son, he

is bound always to treat every one of his men. This is the only effective, true, or practical RULE which can be given on this point of political economy.

And as the captain of a ship is bound to be the last man to leave his ship in case of wreck, and to share his last crust with the sailors in case of famine, so the manufacturer, in any commercial crisis or distress, is bound to take the suffering of it with his men, and even to take more of it for himself than he allows his men to feel; as a father would in a famine, shipwreck, or battle, sacrifice himself for his son.

25. All which sounds very strange: the only real strangeness in the matter being, nevertheless, that it should so sound. For all this is true, and that not partially nor theoretically, but everlastingly and practically: all other doctrine than this respecting matters political being false in premises, absurd in deduction, and impossible in practice, consistently with any progressive state of national life; all the life which we now possess as a nation showing itself in the resolute denial and scorn, by a few strong minds and faithful hearts, of the economic principles taught to our multitudes, which principles, so far as accepted, lead straight to national destruction. Respecting the modes and forms of destruction to which they lead, and, on the other hand, respecting the farther practical working of true polity, I hope to reason farther in a following paper.

Essay II

THE VEINS OF WEALTH

26. The answer which would be made by any ordinary political economist to the statements contained in the preceding paper, is in few words as follows:—

"It is indeed true that certain advantages of a general nature may be obtained by the development of social affections. But political economists never professed, nor profess, to take advantages of a general nature into consideration. Our science is simply the science of getting rich. So far from being a fallacious or visionary one, it is found by experience to be practically effective. Persons who follow its precepts do actually become rich, and persons who disobey them become poor. Every capitalist of Europe has acquired his fortune by following the known laws of our science, and increases his capital daily by an adherence to them. It is vain to bring forward tricks of logic, against the force of accomplished facts. Every man of business knows by experience how money is made, and how it is lost."

Pardon me. Men of business do indeed know how they themselves made their money, or how, on occasion, they lost it. Playing a long-practised game, they are familiar with the chances of its cards, and can rightly explain their losses and gains. But they neither know who keeps the bank of the gambling-house, nor what other games may be played with the same cards, nor what other losses and gains, far away among the dark streets, are essentially, though invisibly, dependent on theirs in the lighted rooms. They have learned a few, and only a few, of the laws of mercantile economy; but not one of those of political economy.

27. Primarily, which is very notable and curious, I observe that men of business rarely know the meaning of the word "rich." At least, if they know, they do not in their reasonings allow for the fact, that it is a relative word, implying its opposite "poor" as positively as the word "north" implies its opposite "south." Men nearly always speak and write as if riches were absolute, and it were possible, by following certain scientific precepts, for everybody to be rich. Whereas riches are a power like that of electricity, acting only through inequalities or negations of itself. The force of the guinea you have in your pocket depends wholly on the default of a guinea in your neighbour's pocket. If he did not want it, it would be of no use to you; the degree of power it possesses depends accurately upon the need or desire he has for it,—and the art of making yourself rich, in the ordinary mercantile economist's sense, is therefore equally and necessarily the art of keeping your neighbour poor.

I would not contend in this matter (and rarely in any matter) for the acceptance of terms. But I wish the reader clearly and deeply to understand the difference between the two economies, to which the terms "Political" and "Mercantile" might not unadvisedly be attached.

28. Political economy (the economy of a State, or of citizens) consists simply in the production, preserva-

tion, and distribution, at fittest time and place, of useful or pleasurable things. The farmer who cuts his hay at the right time; the shipwright who drives his bolts well home in sound wood; the builder who lays good bricks in well-tempered mortar; the housewife who takes care of her furniture in the parlour, and guards against all waste in her kitchen; and the singer who rightly disciplines, and never overstrains her voice, are all political economists in the true and final sense: adding continually to the riches and well-being of the nation to which they belong.

But mercantile economy, the economy of "merces" or of "pay," signifies the accumulation, in the hands of individuals, of legal or moral claim upon, or power over, the labour of others; every such claim implying precisely as much poverty or debt on one side, as it implies riches or right on the other.

It does not, therefore, necessarily involve an addition to the actual property, or well-being of the State in which it exists. But since this commercial wealth, or power over labour, is nearly always convertible at once into real property, while real property is not always convertible at once into power over labour, the idea of riches among active men in civilized nations generally refers to commercial wealth; and in estimating their possessions, they rather calculate the value of their horses and fields by the number of guineas they could get for them, than the value of their guineas by the number of horses and fields they could buy with them.

29. There is, however, another reason for this habit of mind: namely, that an accumulation of real property is of little use to its owner, unless, together with it, he has commercial power over labour. Thus, suppose any

person to be put in possession of a large estate of fruitful land, with rich beds of gold in its gravel; countless herds of cattle in its pastures; houses, and gardens, and storehouses full of useful stores: but suppose, after all, that he could get no servants? In order that he may be able to have servants, some one in his neighbourhood must be poor, and in want of his gold—or his corn. Assume that no one is in want of either, and that no servants are to be had. He must, therefore, bake his own bread, make his own clothes, plough his own ground, and shepherd his own flocks. His gold will be as useful to him as any other yellow pebbles on his estate. His stores must rot, for he cannot consume them. He can eat no more than another man could eat, and wear no more than another man could wear. He must lead a life of severe and common labour to procure even ordinary comforts; he will be ultimately unable to keep either houses in repair, or fields in cultivation; and forced to content himself with a poor man's portion of cottage and garden, in the midst of a desert of waste land, trampled by wild cattle, and encumbered by ruins of palaces, which he will hardly mock at himself by calling "his own."

30. The most covetous of mankind would, with small exultation, I presume, accept riches of this kind on these terms. What is really desired, under the name of riches, is, essentially, power over men; in its simplest sense, the power of obtaining for our own advantage the labour of servant, tradesman, and artist; in wider sense, authority of directing large masses of the nation to various ends (good, trivial, or hurtful, according to the mind of the rich person). And this power of wealth of course is greater or less in direct

proportion to the poverty of the men over whom it is exercised, and in inverse proportion to the number of persons who are as rich as ourselves, and who are ready to give the same price for an article of which the supply is limited. If the musician is poor, he will sing for small pay, as long as there is only one person who can pay him; but if there be two or three, he will sing for the one who offers him most. And thus the power of the riches of the patron (always imperfect and doubtful, as we shall see presently even when most authoritative) depends first on the poverty of the artist, and then on the limitation of the number of equally wealthy persons, who also want seats at the concert. So that, as above stated, the art of becoming "rich," in the common sense, is not absolutely nor finally the art of accumulating much money for ourselves, but also of contriving that our neighbours shall have less. In accurate terms, it is "the art of establishing the maximum inequality in our own favour."

31. Now, the establishment of such inequality cannot be shown in the abstract to be either advantageous or disadvantageous to the body of the nation. The rash and absurd assumption that such inequalities are necessarily advantageous, lies at the root of most of the popular fallacies on the subject of political economy. For the eternal and inevitable law in this matter is, that the beneficialness of the inequality depends, first, on the methods by which it was accomplished; and, secondly, on the purposes to which it is applied. Inequalities of wealth, unjustly established, have assuredly injured the nation in which they exist during their establishment; and, unjustly directed, injure it yet more during their existence. But in-

equalities of wealth, justly established, benefit the nation in the course of their establishment; and, nobly used, aid it yet more by their existence. That is to say, among every active and well-governed people, the various strength of individuals, tested by full exertion and specially applied to various need, issues in unequal, but harmonious results, receiving reward or authority according to its class and service; while, in the inactive or ill-governed nation, the gradations of decay and the victories of treason work out also their own rugged system of subjection and success; and substitute, for the melodious inequalities of concurrent power, the iniquitous dominances and depressions of guilt and misfortune.

32. Thus the circulation of wealth in a nation resembles that of the blood in the natural body. There is one quickness of the current which comes of cheerful emotion or wholesome exercise; and another which comes of shame or of fever. There is a flush of the body which is full of warmth and life; and another which will pass into putrefaction.

The analogy will hold down even to minute particulars. For as diseased local determination of the blood involves depression of the general health of the system, all morbid local action of riches will be found ultimately to involve a weakening of the resources of the body politic.

The mode in which this is produced may be at once understood by examining one or two instances of the development of wealth in the simplest possible circumstances.

33. Suppose two sailors cast away on an uninhabited coast, and obliged to maintain themselves there by their own labour for a series of years.

If they both kept their health, and worked steadily and in amity with each other, they might build themselves a convenient house, and in time come to possess a certain quantity of cultivated land, together with various stores laid up for future use. All these things would be real riches or property; and, supposing the men both to have worked equally hard, they would each have right to equal share or use of it. Their political economy would consist merely in careful preservation and just division of these possessions. Perhaps, however, after some time one or other might be dissatisfied with the results of their common farming; and they might in consequence agree to divide the land they had brought under the spade into equal shares, so that each might thenceforward work in his own field, and live by it. Suppose that after this arrangement had been made, one of them were to fall ill, and be unable to work on his land at a critical time—say of sowing or harvest.

He would naturally ask the other to sow or reap for him.

Then his companion might say, with perfect justice, "I will do this additional work for you; but if I do it, you must promise to do as much for me at another time. I will count how many hours I spend on your ground, and you shall give me a written promise to work for the same number of hours on mine, whenever I need your help, and you are able to give it."

34. Suppose the disabled man's sickness to continue, and that under various circumstances, for several years, requiring the help of the other, he on each occasion gave a written pledge to work, as soon as he was able, at his companion's orders, for the same number of hours which the other had given up to

him. What will the positions of the two men be when the invalid is able to resume work?

Considered as a "Polis," or state, they will be poorer than they would have been otherwise: poorer by the withdrawal of what the sick man's labour would have produced in the interval. His friend may perhaps have toiled with an energy quickened by the enlarged need, but in the end his own land and property must have suffered by the withdrawal of so much of his time and thought from them: and the united property of the two men will be certainly less than it would have been if both had remained in health and activity.

But the relations in which they stand to each other are also widely altered. The sick man has not only pledged his labour for some years, but will probably have exhausted his own share of the accumulated stores, and will be in consequence for some time dependent on the other for food, which he can only "pay" or reward him for by yet more deeply pledging his own labour.

Supposing the written promises to be held entirely valid (among civilized nations their validity is secured by legal measures), the person who had hitherto worked for both might now, if he chose, rest altogether, and pass his time in idleness, not only forcing his companion to redeem all the engagements he had already entered into, but exacting from him pledges for further labour, to an arbitrary amount, for what food he had to advance to him.

35. There might not, from first to last, be the least illegality (in the ordinary sense of the word) in the arrangement; but if a stranger arrived on the coast at this advanced epoch of their political economy, he

would find one man commercially Rich; the other commercially Poor. He would see, perhaps, with no small surprise, one passing his days in idleness; the other labouring for both, and living sparely, in the hope of recovering his independence at some distant period.

This is, of course, an example of one only out of many ways in which inequality of possession may be established between different persons, giving rise to the Mercantile forms of Riches and Poverty. In the instance before us, one of the men might from the first have deliberately chosen to be idle, and to put his life in pawn for present ease; or he might have mismanaged his land, and been compelled to have recourse to his neighbour for food and help, pledging his future labour for it. But what I want the reader to note especially is the fact, common to a large number of typical cases of this kind, that the establishment of the mercantile wealth which consists in a claim upon labour, signifies a political diminution of the real wealth which consists in substantial possessions.

36. Take another example, more consistent with the ordinary course of affairs of trade. Suppose that three men, instead of two, formed the little isolated republic, and found themselves obliged to separate, in order to farm different pieces of land at some distance from each other along the coast: each estate furnishing a distinct kind of produce, and each more or less in need of the material raised on the other. Suppose that the third man, in order to save the time of all three, undertakes simply to superintend the transference of commodities from one farm to the other; on condition of receiving some sufficiently remunerative share of every parcel of goods conveyed, or of some other parcel received in exchange for it.

If this carrier or messenger always brings to each estate, from the other, what is chiefly wanted, at the right time, the operations of the two farmers will go on prosperously, and the largest possible result in produce, or wealth, will be attained by the little community. But suppose no intercourse between the landowners is possible, except through the travelling agent; and that, after a time, this agent, watching the course of each man's agriculture, keeps back the articles with which he has been entrusted until there comes a period of extreme necessity for them, on one side or other, and then exacts in exchange for them all that the distressed farmer can spare of other kinds of produce: it is easy to see that by ingeniously watching his opportunities, he might possess himself regularly of the greater part of the superfluous produce of the two estates, and at last, in some year of severest trial or scarcity, purchase both for himself and maintain the former proprietors thenceforward as his labourers or servants.

37. This would be a case of commercial wealth acquired on the exactest principles of modern political economy. But more distinctly even than in the former instance, it is manifest in this that the wealth of the State, or of the three men considered as a society, is collectively less than it would have been had the merchant been content with juster profit. The operations of the two agriculturists have been cramped to the utmost; and the continual limitations of the supply of things they wanted at critical times, together with the failure of courage consequent on the prolongation of a struggle for mere existence, without any sense of permanent gain, must have seriously diminished the effective results of their labour; and the stores

finally accumulated in the merchant's hand will not
in any wise be of equivalent value to those which,
had his dealings been honest, would have filled at
once the granaries of the farmers and his own. The
whole question, therefore, respecting not only the
advantage, but even the quantity, of national wealth,
resolves itself finally into one of abstract justice. It is
impossible to conclude, of any given mass of acquired
wealth, merely by the fact of its existence, whether
it signifies good or evil to the nation in the midst of
which it exists. Its real value depends on the moral
sign attached to it, just as sternly as that of a mathe-
matical quantity depends on the algebraical sign
attached to it. Any given accumulation of commercial
wealth may be indicative, on the one hand, of faithful
industries, progressive energies, and productive in-
genuities: or, on the other, it may be indicative of
mortal luxury, merciless tyranny, ruinous chicane.
Some treasures are heavy with human tears, as an
ill-stored harvest with untimely rain; and some gold
is brighter in sunshine than it is in substance.

38. And these are not, observe, merely moral or
pathetic attributes of riches, which the seeker of riches
may, if he chooses, despise; they are, literally and
sternly, material attributes of riches, depreciating
or exalting, incalculably, the monetary signification of
the sum in question. One mass of money is the outcome of action which has created,—another, of action
which has annihilated,—ten times as much in the
gathering of it; such and such strong hands have been
paralyzed, as if they had been numbed by nightshade:
so many strong men's courage broken, so many productive operations hindered; this and the other false
direction given to labour, and lying image of prosperity

set up, on Dura plains[1] dug into seven-times-heated furnaces. That which seems to be wealth may in verity be only the gilded index of far-reaching ruin; a wrecker's handful of coin gleaned from the beach to which he has beguiled an argosy; a camp-follower's bundle of rags unwrapped from the breasts of goodly soldiers dead; the purchase-pieces of potter's fields, wherein shall be buried together the citizen and the stranger.[2]

And therefore, the idea that directions can be given for the gaining of wealth, irrespectively of the consideration of its moral sources, or that any general or technical law of purchase and gain can be set down for national practice, is perhaps the most insolently futile of all that ever beguiled men through their vices. So far as I know, there is not in history record of anything so disgraceful to the human intellect as the modern idea that the commercial text, "Buy in the cheapest market and sell in the dearest," represents, or under any circumstances could represent, and available principle of national economy. Buy in the cheapest market?—yes; but what made your market cheap? Charcoal may be cheap among you roof timbers after a fire, and bricks may be cheap in your streets after an earthquake; but fire and earthquake may not therefore be national benefits. Sell in the dearest?—yes, truly; but what made your market dear? You sold your bread well to-day: was it to a dying man who gave his last coin for it, and will never need bread more; or to a rich man who to-morrow will buy your farm over your head; or to a soldier on his way to pillage the bank in which you have put your fortune?

[1] Cf. Daniel 3:1.
[2] Cf. Matthew 27:6-7.

None of these things you can know. One thing only you can know: namely, whether this dealing of yours is a just and faithful one, which is all you need concern yourself about respecting it; sure thus to have done your own part in bringing about ultimately in the world a state of things which will not issue in pillage or in death. And thus every question concerning these things merges itself ultimately in the great question of justice, which, the ground being thus far cleared for it, I will enter upon in the next paper, leaving only, in this, three final points for the reader's consideration.

39. It has been shown that the chief value and virtue of money consists in its having power over human beings; that, without this power, large material possesssions are useless, and to any person possessing such power, comparatively unnecessary. But power over human beings is attainable by other means than by money. As I said a few pages back, the money power is always imperfect and doubtful; there are many things which cannot be reached with it, others which cannot be retained by it. Many joys may be given to men which cannot be bought for gold, and many fidelities found in them which cannot be rewarded with it.

Trite enough,—the reader thinks. Yes: but it is not so trite,—I wish it were,—that in this moral power, quite inscrutable and immeasurable though it be, there is a monetary value just as real as that represented by more ponderous currencies. A man's hand may be full of invisible gold, and the wave of it, or the grasp, shall do more than another's with a shower of bullion. This invisible gold, also, does not necessarily diminish in spending. Political economists will do well some day to take heed of it, though they cannot take measure.

But farther. Since the essence of wealth consists in its authority over men, if the apparent or nominal wealth fail in this power, it fails in essence; in fact, ceases to be wealth at all. It does not appear lately in England, that our authority over men is absolute. The servants show some disposition to rush riotously up-stairs, under an impression that their wages are not regularly paid. We should augur ill of any gentleman's property to whom this happened every other day in his drawing-room.

So, also, the power of our wealth seems limited as respects the comfort of the servants, no less than their quietude. The persons in the kitchen appear to be ill-dressed, squalid, half-starved. One cannot help imagining that the riches of the establishment must be of a very theoretical and documentary character.

40. Finally. Since the essence of wealth consists in power over men, will it not follow that the nobler and the more in number the persons are over whom it has power, the greater the wealth? Perhaps it may even appear, after some consideration, that the persons themselves *are* the wealth—that these pieces of gold with which we are in the habit of guiding them, are, in fact, nothing more than a kind of Byzantine harness or trappings, very glittering and beautiful in barbaric sight, wherewith we bridle the creatures; but that if these same living creatures could be guided without the fretting and jingling of the Byzants[3] in their mouths and ears, they might themselves be more valuable than their bridles. In fact, it may be discovered that the true veins of wealth are purple—and not in Rock, but in Flesh—perhaps even that the final

[3] Gold coins.

outcome and consummation of all wealth is in the
producing as many as possible full-breathed, bright-
eyed, and happy-hearted human creatures. Our modern wealth, I think, has rather a tendency the other
way;—most political economists appearing to consider
multitudes of human creatures not conducive to
wealth, or at best conducive to it only by remaining
in a dim-eyed and narrow-chested state of being.

41. Nevertheless, it is open, I repeat, to serious question, which I leave to the reader's pondering, whether,
among national manufactures, that of Souls of a good
quality may not at last turn out a quite leadingly
lucrative one? Nay, in some far-away and yet un-
dreamt-of hour, I can even imagine that England may
cast all thoughts of possessive wealth back to the
barbaric nations among whom they first arose; and
that, while the sands of the Indus and adamant of
Golconda may yet stiffen the housings of the charger,
and flash from the turban of a slave, she, as a Christian
mother, may at last attain to the virtues and the treasures of a Heathen one, and be able to lead forth her
Sons, saying,—

"These are MY Jewels." [4]

[4] For clarification of the latter part of this paragraph, see, in
the writings of Valerius Maximus, the introduction to "De
Paupertate" which comes in the fourth part of Book IV.

Essay III

QUI JUDICATIS TERRAM?[1]

42. Some centuries before the Christian era, a Jew merchant, largely engaged in business on the Gold Coast, and reported to have made one of the largest fortunes of his time (held also in repute for much practical sagacity), left among his ledgers some general maxims concerning wealth, which have been preserved, strangely enough, even to our own days. They were held in considerable respect by the most active traders of the Middle Ages, especially by the Venetians, who even went so far in their admiration as to place a statue of the old Jew on the angle of one of their principal public buildings.[2] Of late years these writings have fallen into disrepute, being opposed in every particular to the spirit of modern commerce. Nevertheless I shall reproduce a passage or two from them here, partly because they may interest the reader by their novelty; and chiefly because they will show him that it is possible for a very practical and acquisitive tradesman to hold, through a not unsuccessful career, that principle of distinction between well-gotten and ill-gotten wealth, which, partially insisted on in my last paper, it must be our work more completely to examine in this.

[1] For an explanation of this title see Paragraph 46.
[2] Ruskin refers to the sculpture of Solomon on the Ducal Palace. See *The Stones of Venice* (*Works*, X, 359, 363) for further allusions.

45

43.[3] He says, for instance, in one place: "The getting of treasures by a lying tongue is a vainty tossed to and fro of them that seek death";[4] adding in another, with the same meaning (he has a curious way of doubling his sayings): "Treasures of wickedness profit nothing: but justice delivers from death." Both these passages are notable for their assertions of death as the only real issue and sum of attainment by any unjust scheme of wealth. If we read, instead of "lying tongue," "lying label, title, pretence, or advertisement," we shall more clearly perceive the bearing of the words on modern business. The seeking of death is a grand expression of the true course of men's toil in such business. We usually speak as if death pursued us, and we fled from him; but that is only so in rare instances. Ordinarily he masks himself—makes himself beautiful—all-glorious; not like the King's daughter, all-glorious within, but outwardly: his clothing of wrought gold. We pursue him frantically all our days, he flying or hiding from us. Our crowning success at three-score and ten is utterly and perfectly to seize, and hold him in his eternal integrity—robes, ashes, and sting.

Again: the merchant says, "He that oppresseth the poor to increase his riches, shall surely come to want." And again, more strongly: "Rob not the poor because he is poor; neither oppress the afflicted in the place of business. For God shall spoil the soul of those that spoiled them."

This "robbing the poor because he is poor," is especially the mercantile form of theft, consisting in

[3] Paragraphs 43 and 44—particularly the former—derive from passages in the Authorized Version, the Vulgate, and the Apocrypha.
[4] Proverbs 21:6.

taking advantage of a man's necessities in order to obtain his labour or property at a reduced price. The ordinary highwayman's opposite form of robbery—of the rich, because he is rich—does not appear to occur so often to the old merchant's mind; probably because, being less profitable and more dangerous than the robbery of the poor, it is rarely practised by persons of discretion.

44. But the two most remarkable passages in their deep general significance are the following:—

"The rich and the poor have met. God is their maker."

"The rich and the poor have met. God is their light."

They "have met": more literally, have stood in each other's way (*obviaverunt*). That is to say, as long as the world lasts, the action and counteraction of wealth and poverty, the meeting, face to face, of rich and poor, is just as appointed and necessary a law of that world as the flow of stream to sea, or the interchange of power among the electric clouds:—"God is their maker." But, also, this action may be either gentle and just, or convulsive and destructive: it may be by rage of devouring flood, or by lapse of serviceable wave;—in blackness of thunderstroke, or continual force of vital fire, soft, and shapeable into love-syllables from far away. And which of these it shall be, depends on both rich and poor knowing that God is their light; that in the mystery of human life, there is no other light than this by which they can see each other's faces, and live;—light, which is called in another of the books among which the merchant's maxims have been preserved, the "sun of justice," of which it is promised that it shall rise at last with "healing" (health-giving or helping, making whole or setting at one) in its wings. For truly this healing is only possible by means of justice; no love, no faith, no hope will do it; men will be unwisely fond—vainly faithful,—unless primarily they are just; and the mistake of the best men through generation after generation, has been that great one of thinking to help the poor by almsgiving, and by preaching of patience or of hope, and by every other means, emollient or consolatory, except the one thing which God orders for them, justice. But this justice, with its accompanying holiness or helpfulness, being even by the best man denied in its trial time, is by the mass of men hated wherever it appears: so that, when the choice was one day fairly put to them, they denied the Helpful One and the Just; and desired a murderer, sedition-raiser, and robber, to be granted to them;—the murderer instead of the Lord of Life, the sedition-raiser instead of the Prince of Peace, and the robber instead of the Just Judge of all the world.

45. I have just spoken of the flowing of streams to the sea as a partial image of the action of wealth. In one respect it is not a partial, but a perfect image. The popular economist thinks himself wise in having discovered that wealth, or the forms of property in general, must go where they are required; that where demand is, supply must follow. He farther declares that this course of demand and supply cannot be forbidden by human laws. Precisely in the same sense, and with the same certainty, the waters of the world go where they are required. Where the land falls, the water flows. The course neither of clouds nor rivers can be forbidden by human will. But the disposition and administration of them can be altered by human forethought. Whether the stream shall be a curse or a

blessing, depends upon man's labour, and administering intelligence. For centuries after centuries, great districts of the world, rich in soil, and favoured in climate, have lain desert under the rage of their own rivers; nor only desert, but plague-struck. The stream which, rightly directed, would have flowed in soft irrigation from field to field—would have purified the air, given food to man and beast, and carried their burdens for them on its bosom—now overwhelms the plain and poisons the wind; its breath pestilence, and its work famine. In like manner this wealth "goes where it is required." No human laws can withstand its flow. They can only guide it: but this, the leading trench and limiting mound can do so thoroughly, that it shall become water of life—the riches of the hand of wisdom; or, on the contrary, by leaving it to its own lawless flow, they may make it, what it has been too often, the last and deadliest of national plagues: water of Marah[5]—the water which feeds the roots of all evil.

The necessity of these laws of distribution or restaint is curiously overlooked in the ordinary political economist's definition of his own "science." He calls it, shortly, the "science of getting rich." But there are many sciences, as well as many arts, of getting rich. Poisoning people of large estates, was one employed largely in the Middle Ages; adulteration of food of people of small estates, is one employed largely now. The ancient and honourable Highland method of black mail; the more modern and less honourable system of obtaining goods on credit,[6] and the other variously improved methods of appropriation—which,

[5] Exodus 15:23.
[6] Ruskin belabors the credit system frequently in his writings.

in major and minor scales of industry, down to the
most artistic pocket-picking, we owe to recent genius,
—all come under the general head of sciences, or
arts, of getting rich.

46. So that it is clear the popular economist, in calling his science the science par excellence of getting
rich, must attach some peculiar ideas of limitation
to its character. I hope I do not misrepresent him,
by assuming that he means *his* science to be the
science of "getting rich by legal or just means." In
this definition, is the word "just," or "legal," finally
to stand? For it is possible among certain nations,
or under certain rulers, or by help of certain advocates,
that proceedings may be legal which are by no means
just. If, therefore, we leave at last only the word "just"
in that place of our definition, the insertion of this
solitary and small word will make a notable difference
in the grammar of our science. For then it will follow
that in order to grow rich scientifically, we must grow
rich justly; and, therefore, know what is just; so that
our economy will no longer depend merely on prudence, but on jurisprudence—and that of divine, not
human law. Which prudence is indeed of no mean
order, holding itself, as it were, high in the air of
heaven, and gazing for ever on the light of the sun
of justice; hence the souls which have excelled in it
are represented by Dante as stars forming in heaven
for ever the figure of the eye of an eagle;[7] they having
been in life the discerners of light from darkness; or
to the whole human race, as the light of the body,
which is the eye;[8] while those souls which form the

[7] Cf. Paradiso, Canto 18.
[8] Cf. Matthew 6:22.

wings of the bird (giving power and dominion to justice, "healing in its wings") trace also in light the inscription in heaven: "DILIGITE JUSTITIAM QUI JUDICATIS TERRAM." "Ye who judge the earth, give" (not, observe, merely love, but) "diligent love to justice": the love which seeks diligently, that is to say, choosingly, and by preference to all things else. Which judging or doing judgment in the earth is, according to their capacity and position, required not of judges only, nor of rulers only, but of all men: a truth sorrowfully lost sight of even by those who are ready enough to apply to themselves passages in which Christian men are spoken of as called to be "saints" (*i.e.*, to helpful or healing functions); and "chosen to be kings" [9] (*i.e.*, to knowing or directing functions); the true meaning of these titles having been long lost through the pretences of unhelpful and unable persons to saintly and kingly character; also through the once popular idea that both the sanctity and royalty are to consist in wearing long robes and high crowns, instead of in mercy and judgment; whereas all true sanctity is saving power, as all true royalty is ruling power; and injustice is part and parcel of the denial of such power, which "makes men as the creeping things, as the fishes of the sea, that have no ruler over them."

47. Absolute justice is indeed no more attainable than absolute truth; but the righteous man is distinguished from the unrighteous by his desire and hope of justice, as the true man from the false by his desire and hope of truth. And though absolute justice be

---

[9] From here to the end of the paragraph is a tissue of Biblical adaptations: from Romans, Revelation, Psalms, and Habakkuk.

unattainable, as much justice as we need for all practical use is attainable by all those who make it their aim.

We have to examine, then, in the subject before us, what are the laws of justice respecting payment of labour—no small part, these, of the foundations of all jurisprudence.

I reduced, in my last paper, the idea of money payment to its simplest or radical terms. In those terms its nature, and the conditions of justice respecting it, can be best ascertained.

Money payment, as there stated, consists radically in a promise to some person working for us, that for the time and labour he spends in our service to-day we will give or procure equivalent time and labour in his service at any future time when he may demand it.

If we promise to give him less labour than he has given us, we under-pay him. If we promise to give him more labour than he has given us, we over-pay him. In practice, according to the laws of demand and supply, when two men are ready to do the work, and only one man wants to have it done, the two men underbid each other for it; and the one who gets it to do, is under-paid. But when two men want the work done, and there is only one man ready to do it, the two men who want it done overbid each other, and the workman is over-paid.

48. I will examine these two points of injustice in succession; but first I wish the reader to clearly understand the central principle, lying between the two, of right or just payment.

When we ask a service of any man, he may either give it us freely, or demand payment for it. Respecting free gift of service, there is no question at present,

that being a matter of affection—not of traffic. But if
he demand payment for it, and we wish to treat him
with absolute equity, it is evident that this equity
can only consist in giving time for time, strength for
strength, and skill for skill. If a man works an hour
for us, and we only promise to work half an hour for
him in return, we obtain an unjust advantage. If, on
the contrary, we promise to work an hour and a half
for him in return, he has an unjust advantage. The
justice consists in absolute exchange; or, if there be
any respect to the stations of the parties, it will not
be in favour of the employer: there is certainly no
equitable reason in a man's being poor, that if he give
me a pound of bread to-day, I should return him less
than a pound of bread to-morrow; or any equitable
reason in a man's being uneducated, that if he uses a
certain quantity of skill and knowledge in my service,
I should use a less quantity of skill and knowledge in
his. Perhaps, ultimately, it may appear desirable, or,
to say the least, gracious, that I should give in return
somewhat more than I received. But at present, we are
concerned on the law of justice only, which is that of
perfect and accurate exchange;—one circumstance
only interfering with the simplicity of this radical
idea of just payment—that inasmuch as labour
(rightly directed) is fruitful just as seed is, the fruit
(or "interest," as it is called) of the labour first given,
or "advanced," ought to be taken into account, and
balanced by an additional quantity of labour in the
subsequent repayment. Supposing the repayment to
take place at the end of the year, or of any other given
time, this calculation could be approximately made,
but as money (that is to say, cash) payment involves
no reference to time (it being optional with the per-

son paid to spend what he receives at once or after any number of years), we can only assume, generally, that some slight advantage must in equity be allowed to the person who advances the labour, so that the typical form of bargain will be: if you give me an hour to-day, I will give you an hour and five minutes on demand. If you give me a pound of bread to-day, I will give you seventeen ounces on demand, and so on. All that is necessary for the reader to note is, that the amount returned is at least in equity not to be *less* than the amount given.

The abstract idea, then, of just or due wages, as respects the labourer, is that they will consist in a sum of money which will at any time procure for him at least as much labour as he has given, rather more than less. And this equity or justice of payment is, observe, wholly independent of any reference to the number of men who are willing to do the work. I want a horseshoe for my horse. Twenty smiths, or twenty thousand smiths, may be ready to forge it; their number does not in one atom's weight affect the question of the equitable payment of the one who *does* forge it. It costs him a quarter of an hour of his life, and so much skill and strength of arm, to make that horseshoe for me. Then at some future time I am bound in equity to give a quarter of an hour, and some minutes more, of my life (or of some other person's at my disposal), and also as much strength of arm and skill, and a little more, in making or doing what the smith may have need of.

49. Such being the abstract theory of just remunerative payment, its application is practically modified by the fact that the order for labor, given in payment, is general, while the labour received is special. The

current coin or document is practically an order on
the nation for so much work of any kind; and this
universal applicability to immediate need renders it
so much more valuable than special labour can be,
that an order for a less quantity of this general toil
will always be accepted as a just equivalent for a
greater quantity of special toil. Any given craftsman
will always be willing to give an hour of his own
work in order to receive command over half an hour,
or even much less, of national work. This source of
uncertainty, together with the difficulty of determining the monetary value of skill,[10] render the ascertain-
ment (even approximate) of the proper wages of any
given labour in terms of a currency, matter of considerable complexity. But they do not affect the principle of exchange. The worth of the work may not be
easily known; but it *has* a worth, just as fixed and
real as the specific gravity of a substance, though such
specific gravity may not be easily ascertainable when
the substance is untied with many others. Nor is there
so much difficulty or chance in determining it, as in
determining the ordinary maxima and minima of vul-
gar political economy. There are few bargains in
which the buyer can ascertain with anything like
precision that the seller would have taken no less;—or
the seller acquire more than a comfortable faith that
the purchaser would have given no more. This impossibility of precise knowledge prevents neither from
striving to attain the desired point of greatest vex-

---

[10] In a lengthy note (*Works*, XVII, 67) Ruskin defines skill as
"the united force of experience, intellect, and passion, in their
operation on manual labour: and under the term 'passion' to
include the entire range and agency of the moral feelings. . . ."
He then berates John Stuart Mill for failing, in the *Principles of
Political Economy*, to give sufficient attention to feeling.

ation and injury to the other, nor from accepting it for a scientific principle that he is to buy for the least and sell for the most possible, though what the real least or most may be he cannot tell. In like manner, a just person lays it down for a scientific principle that he is to pay a just price, and, without being able precisely to ascertain the limits of such a price, will nevertheless strive to attain the closest possible approximation to them. A practically serviceable approximation he *can* obtain. It is easier to determine scientifically what a man ought to have for his work, than what his necessities will compel him to take for it. His necessities can only be ascertained by empirical, but his due by analytical, investigation. In the one case, you try your answer to the sum like a puzzled schoolboy—till you find one that fits; in the other, you bring out your result within certain limits, by process of calculation.

50. Supposing, then, the just wages of any quantity of given labour to have been ascertained, let us examine the first results of just and unjust payment, when in favour of the purchaser or employer: *i.e.*, when two men are ready to do the work, and only one wants to have it done.

The unjust purchaser forces the two to bid against each other till he has reduced their demand to its lowest terms. Let us assume that the lowest bidder offers to do the work at half its just price.

The purchaser employs him, and does not employ the other. The first or *apparent* result is, therefore, that one of the two men is left out of employ, or to starvation, just as definitely as by the just procedure of giving fair price to the best workman. The various writers who endeavoured to invalidate the positions of my first paper never saw this, and assumed that the unjust hirer employed *both*. He employs both no more than the just hirer. The only difference (in the outset) is that the just man pays sufficiently, the unjust man insufficiently, for the labour of the single person employed.

I say, "in the outset"; for this first or apparent difference is not the actual difference. By the unjust procedure, half the proper price of the work is left in the hand of the employer. This enables him to hire another man at the same unjust rate, on some other kind of work; and the final result is that he has two men working for him at half-price, and two are out of employ.

51. By the just procedure, the whole price of the first piece of work goes into the hands of the man who does it. No surplus being left in the employer's hands, *he* cannot hire another man for another piece of labour. But by precisely so much as his power is diminished, the hired workman's power is increased: that is to say, by the additional half of the price he has received; which additional half *he* has the power of using to employ another man in *his* service. I will suppose, for the moment, the least favourable, though quite probable, case—that, though justly treated himself, he yet will act unjustly to his subordinate; and hire at half-price if he can. The final result will then be, that one man works for the employer, at just price; one for the workman, at half-price; and two, as in the first case, are still out of employ. These two, as I said before, are out of employ in *both* cases. The difference between the just and unjust procedure does not lie in the number of men hired, but in the price paid to them, and the *persons by whom* it is paid. The es-

sential difference, that which I want the reader to see clearly, is, that in the unjust case, two men work for one, the first hirer. In the just case, one man works for the first hirer, one for the person hired, and so on, down or up through the various grades of service; the influence being carried forward by justice, and arrested by injustice. The universal and constant action of justice in this matter is therefore to diminish the power of wealth, in the hands of one individual, over masses of men, and to distribute it through a chain of men. The actual power exerted by the wealth is the same in both cases; but by injustice it is put all into one man's hands, so that he directs at once and with equal force the labour of a circle of men about him; by the just procedure, he is permitted to touch the nearest only, through whom, with diminished force, modified by new minds, the energy of the wealth passes on to others, and so till it exhausts itself.

52. The immediate operation of justice in this respect is therefore to diminish the power of wealth, first, in acquisition of luxury, and secondly, in exercise of moral influence. The employer cannot concentrate so multitudinous labour on his own interests, nor can he subdue so multitudinous mind to his own will. But the secondary operation of justice is not less important. The insufficient payment of the group of men working for one, places each under a maximum of difficulty in rising above his position. The tendency of the system is to check advancement. But the sufficient or just payment, distributed through a descending series of offices or grades of labour, gives each subordinated person fair and sufficient means of rising in the social scale, if he chooses to use them; and thus not only

diminishes the immediate power of wealth, but removes the worst disabilities of poverty.

53. It is on this vital problem that the entire destiny of the labourer is ultimately dependent. Many minor interests may sometimes appear to interfere with it, but all branch from it. For instance, considerable agitation is often caused in the minds of the lower classes when they discover the share which they nominally, and to all appearance, actually, pay out of their wages in taxation (I believe thirty-five or forty per cent). This sounds very grievous; but in reality the labourer does not pay it, but his employer. If the workman had not to pay it, his wages would be less by just that sum; competition would still reduce them to the lowest rate at which life was possible. Similarly the lower orders agitated for the repeal of the corn laws, thinking they would be better off if bread were cheaper; never perceiving that as soon as bread was permanently cheaper, wages would permanently fall in precisely that proportion. The corn laws were rightly repealed; not, however, because they directly oppressed the poor, but because they indirectly oppressed them in causing a large quantity of their labour to be consumed unproductively. So also unnecessary taxation oppresses them, through destruction of capital; but the destiny of the poor depends primarily always on this one question of the dueness of wages. Their distress (irrespectively of that caused by sloth, minor error, or crime) arises on the grand scale from the two reacting forces of competition and oppression. There is not yet, nor will yet for ages be, any real over-population in the world; but a local over-population, or, more accurately, a degree of popu-

lation locally unmanageable under existing circumstances for want of forethought and sufficient ma-
chinery, necessarily shows itself by pressure of competition; and the taking advantage of this competition
by the purchaser to obtain their labour unjustly cheap,
consummates at once their suffering and his own; for
in this (as I believe in every other kind of slavery)
the oppressor suffers at last more than the oppressed,
and those magnificent lines of Pope, even in all their
force, fall short of the truth:—

"Yet, to be just to these poor men of pelf,
 Each does but HATE HIS NEIGHBOUR AS HIMSELF:
 Damned to the mines, an equal fate betides
 The slave that digs it, and the slave that hides." [11]

54. The collateral and reversionary operations of
justice in this matter I shall examine hereafter (it
being needful first to define the nature of value); pro-
ceeding then to consider within what practical terms
a juster system may be established; and ultimately the
vexed question of the destinies of the unemployed
workmen. Lest, however, the reader should be alarmed
at some of the issues to which our investigations seem
to be tending, as if in their bearing against the power
of wealth they had something in common with those
of socialism, I wish him to know, in accurate terms,
one or two of the main points which I have in view.

Whether socialism has made more progress among
the army and navy (where payment is made on my
principles), or among the manufacturing operatives
(who are paid on my opponents' principles), I leave
it to those opponents to ascertain and declare. Whatever their conclusion may be, I think it necessary to

[11] "Moral Essays," Epistle iii.

answer for myself only this: that if there be any one point insisted on throughout my works more frequently than another, that one point is the impossibility of Equality. My continual aim has been to show the eternal superiority of some men to others, sometimes even of one man to all others; and to show also the advisability of appointing such persons or person to guide, to lead, or on occasion even to compel and subdue, their inferiors according to their own better knowledge and wiser will. My principles of Political Economy were all involved in a single phrase spoken three years ago at Manchester: "Soldiers of the Ploughshare as well as Soldiers of the Sword":[12] and they were all summed in a single sentence in the last volume of *Modern Painters*—"Government and co-operation are in all things the Laws of Life; Anarchy and competition the Laws of Death."

And with respect to the mode in which these general principles affect the secure possession of property, so far am I from invalidating such security, that the whole gist of these papers will be found ultimately to aim at an extension in its range; and whereas it has long been known and declared that the poor have no right to the property of the rich, I wish it also to be known and declared that the rich have no right to the property of the poor.

55. But that the working of the system which I have undertaken to develop would in many ways shorten the apparent and direct, though not the unseen and collateral, power, both of wealth, as the Lady of Pleasure, and of capital as the Lord of Toil, I do not deny: on the contrary, I affirm it in all joyfulness; knowing that the attraction of riches is already too strong, as

[12] In a lecture given on July 10, 1857. See *Works*, XVI, 26.

their authority is already too weighty, for the reason
of mankind. I said in my last paper[13] that nothing in
history had ever been so disgraceful to human intellect as the acceptance among us of the common doc-
trines of political economy as a science. I have many
grounds for saying this, but one of the chief may be
given in few words. I know no previous instance in
history of a nation's establishing a systematic disobedi-
ence to the first principles of its professed religion.
The writings which we (verbally) esteem as divine,
not only denounce the love of money as the source
of all evil,[14] and as an idolatry abhorred of the Deity,
but declare mammon service to be the accurate and
irreconcileable [sic.] opposite of God's service:[15] and,
whenever they speak of riches absolute, and poverty
absolute, declare woe to the rich, and blessing to the
poor. Whereupon we forthwith investigate a science of
becoming rich, as the shortest road to national prosperity.

"Tai Cristian dannerà l'Etiòpe,
  Quando so partiranno i due collegi,
  L'UNO IN ETERNO RICCO, E L'ALTRO INÒPE." [16]

[13] Ruskin slips here. He is referring to his first essay; see opening of "The Roots of Honour."
[14] Cf. I Timothy 6:10.
[15] Cf. Matthew 6:24.
[16] Paradiso, Canto xix. Cary's translation runs:

  Christians like these the Aethiop shall condemn:
  When that the two assemblages shall part;
  One rich eternally, the other poor.

Essay IV

AD VALOREM

56. In the last paper we saw that just payment of labour consisted in a sum of money which would approximately obtain equivalent labour at a future time: we have now to examine the means of obtaining such equivalence. Which question involves the definition of Value, Wealth, Price, and Produce.

None of these terms are yet defined so as to be understood by the public. But the last, Produce, which one might have thought the clearest of all, is, in use, the most ambiguous; and the examination of the kind of ambiguity attendant on its present employment will best open the way to our work.

In his chapter on Capital,[1] Mr. J. S. Mill instances, as a capitalist, a hardware manufacturer, who, having intended to spend a certain portion of the proceeds of his business in buying plate and jewels, changes his mind, and "pays it as wages to additional workpeople." The effect is stated by Mr. Mill to be, that "more food is appropriated to the consumption of productive labourers."

57. Now I do not ask, though, had I written this paragraph, it would surely have been asked of me, What is to become of the silversmiths? If they are truly unproductive persons, we will acquiesce in their extinction. And though in another part of the same passage, the hardware merchant is supposed also to

[1] *Principles of Political Economy*, Book I, ch. iv.

dispense with a number of servants, whose "food is thus set free for productive purposes," I do not inquire what will be the effect, painful or otherwise, upon the servants, of this emancipation of their food. But I very seriously inquire why ironware is produce, and silverware is not? That the merchant consumes the one, and sells the other, certainly does not constitute the difference, unless it can be shown (which, indeed, I perceive it to be becoming daily more and more the aim of tradesmen to show) that commodities are made to be sold, and not to be consumed. The merchant is an agent of conveyance to the consumer in one case, and is himself the consumer in the other: but the labourers are in either case equally productive, since they have produced goods to the same value, if the hardware and the plate are both goods.

And what distinction separates them? It is indeed possible that in the "comparative estimate of the moralist," with which Mr. Mill says political economy has nothing to do (III. i. 2), a steel fork might appear a more substantial production than a silver one: we may grant also that knives, no less than forks, are good produce; and scythes and ploughshares serviceable articles. But, how of bayonets? Supposing the hardware merchant to effect large sales of *these*, by help of the "setting free" of the food of his servants and his silversmith,—is he still employing productive labourers, or, in Mr. Mill's words, labourers who increase "the stock of permanent means of enjoyment" (I. iii. 4)? Or if, instead of bayonets, he supply bombs, will not the absolute and final "enjoyment" of even these energetically productive articles (each of which costs ten pounds) be dependent on a proper choice of time and place for their *enfantement;* choice, that

is to say, depending on those philosophical considerations with which political economy has nothing to do?

58. I should have regretted the need of pointing
out inconsistency in any portion of Mr. Mill's work,
had not the value of his work proceeded from its in-
consistencies. He deserves honour among economists
by inadvertently disclaiming the principles which he
states, and tacitly introducing the moral considerations with which he declares his science has no connection. Many of his chapters are, therefore, true and
valuable; and the only conclusions of his which I have
to dispute are those which follow from his premises.

Thus, the idea which lies at the root of the passage
we have just been examining, namely, that labour applied to produce luxuries will not support so many
persons as labour applied to produce useful articles,
is entirely true; but the instance given fails—and in
four directions of failure at once—because Mr. Mill
has not defined the real meaning of usefulness. The
definition which he has given—"capacity to satisfy a
desire, or serve a purpose" (III. i. 2)—applies equally
to the iron and silver; while the true definition—which
he has not given, but which nevertheless underlies the
false verbal definition in his mind, and comes out
once or twice by accident (as in the words "any support to life or strength" in I. iii. 5)—applies to some
articles of iron, but not to others, and to some articles
of silver, but not to others. It applies to ploughs, but
not to bayonets; and to forks, but not to filigree.

59. The eliciting of the true definitions will give us
the reply to our first question, "What is value?" respecting which, however, we must first hear the popular statements.

"The word 'value,' when used without adjunct, al-

ways means, in political economy, value in exchange"
(Mill, III. i. 2). So that, if two ships cannot exchange
their rudders, their rudders are, in politico-economic
language, of no value to either.

But "the subject of political economy is wealth."—
(Preliminary remarks, page 1.)

And wealth "consists of all useful and agreeable
objects which possess exchangeable value."—(Preliminary remarks, page 10.)

It appears, then, according to Mr. Mill, that usefulness and agreeableness underlie the exchange value,
and must be ascertained to exist in the thing, before
we can esteem it an object of wealth.

Now, the economical usefulness of a thing depends
not merely on its own nature, but on the number of
people who can and will use it. A horse is useless, and
therefore unsaleable, if no one can ride,—a sword,
if no one can strike, and meat, if no one can eat. Thus
every material utility depends on its relative human
capacity.

Similarly: The agreeableness of a thing depends not
merely on its own likeableness, but on the number of
people who can be got to like it. The relative agreeableness, and therefore saleableness, of "a pot of the
smallest ale," and of "Adonis painted by a running
brook," depends virtually on the opinion of Demos,
in the shape of Christopher Sly.[2] That is to say, the
agreeableness of a thing depends on its relatively
human disposition. Therefore, political economy, being a science of wealth, must be a science respecting
human capacities and dispositions. But moral considerations have nothing to do with political economy
(III. i. 2). Therefore, moral considerations have noth-

[2] Cf. The Taming of the Shrew, Induction, sc. ii.

ing to do with human capacities and dispositions.

60. I do not wholly like the look of this conclusion from Mr. Mill's statements:—let us try Mr. Ricardo's.[2]

"Utility is not the measure of exchangeable value, though it is absolutely essential to it."—(Chap. I. sect. i.) Essential in what degree, Mr. Ricardo? There may be greater and less degrees of utility. Meat, for instance, may be so good as to be fit for any one to eat, or so bad as to be fit for no one to eat. What is the exact degree of goodness which is "essential" to its exchangeable value, but not "the measure" of it? How good must the meat be, in order to possess any exchangeable value? and how bad must it be—(I wish this were a settled question in London markets) —in order to possess none?

There appears to be some hitch, I think, in the working even of Mr. Ricardo's principles; but let him take his own example: "Suppose that in the early stages of society the bows and arrows of the hunter were of equal value with the implements of the fisherman. Under such cirmumstances the value of the deer, the produce of the hunter's day's labour, would be *exactly*" (italics mine) "equal to the value of the fish, the product of the fisherman's day's labour. The comparative value of the fish and game would be *entirely* regulated by the quantity of labour realized in each." (Ricardo, chap. iii. On Value.)

Indeed! Therefore, if the fisherman catches one sprat, and the huntsman one deer, one sprat will be equal in value to one deer; but if the fisherman catches no sprat and the huntsman two deer, no sprat will be equal in value to two deer?

Nay; but—Mr. Ricardo's supporters may say—he

[2] *Principles of Political Economy and Taxation.*

means, on an average;—if the average product of a day's work of fisher and hunter be one fish and one deer, the one fish will always be equal in value to the one deer.

Might I inquire the species of fish? Whale? or whitebait?

It would be waste of time to pursue these fallacies farther; we will seek for a true definition.

61. Much store has been set for centuries upon the use of our English classical education. It were to be wished that our well-educated merchants recalled to mind always this much of their Latin schooling,— that the nominative of *valorem* (a word already sufficiently familiar to them) is *valor;* a word which, therefore, ought to be familiar to them. *Valor,* from valere, to be well or strong (ὑγιαίνω);—strong, *in* life (if a man), or valiant; strong, *for* life (if a thing), or valuable. To be "valuable," therefore, is to "avail towards life." A truly valuable or availing thing is that which leads to life with its whole strength. In proportion as it does not lead to life, or as its strength is broken, it is less valuable; in proportion as it leads away from life, it is unvaluable or malignant.

The value of a thing, therefore, is independent of opinion, and of quantity. Think what you will of it, gain how much you may of it, the value of the thing itself is neither greater nor less. For ever it avails, or avails not; no estimate can raise, no disdain repress, the power which it holds from the Maker of things and men.

The real science of political economy, which has yet to be distinguished from the bastard science, as medicine from witchcraft, and astronomy from astrology, is that which teaches nations to desire and labour for the things that lead to life: and which teaches them to scorn and destroy the things that lead to destruction. And if, in a state of infancy, they supposed indifferent things, such as excrescences of shell-fish, and pieces of blue and red stone, to be valuable, and spent large measures of the labour which ought to be employed for the extension and ennobling of life, in diving or digging for them, and cutting them into various shapes,—or if, in the same state of infancy, they imagine precious and beneficent things, such as air, light, and cleanliness, to be valueless,— or if, finally, they imagine the conditions of their own existence, by which alone they can truly possess or use anything, such, for instance, as peace, trust, and love, to be prudently exchangeable, when the markets offer, for gold, iron, or excrescences of shells—the great and only science of Political Economy teaches them, in all these cases, what is vanity, and what substance; and how the service of Death, the Lord of Waste, and of eternal emptiness, differs from the service of Wisdom, the Lady of Saving, and of eternal fullness; she who has said, "I will cause those that love me to inherit SUBSTANCE; and I will FILL their treasures." [4]

The "Lady of Saving," in a profounder sense than that of the savings bank, though that is a good one: Madonna della Salute,[5]—Lady of Health,—which, though commonly spoken of as if separate from wealth, is indeed a part of wealth. This word, "wealth," it will be remembered, is the next we have to define.

62. "To be wealthy," says Mr. Mill, "is to have a large stock of useful articles."

[4] Proverbs 8:21.
[5] Ruskin has in mind Santa Maria della Salute, one of many superb Venetian churches. See also, *Works,* x, 443.

I accept this definition. Only let us perfectly understand it. My opponents often lament my not giving them enough logic: I fear I must at present use a little more than they will like; but this business of Political Economy is no light one, and we must allow no loose terms in it.

We have, therefore, to ascertain in the above definition, first, what is the meaning of "having," or the nature of Possession. Then what is the meaning of "useful," or the nature of Utility.

And first of possession. At the crossing of the transepts of Milan Cathedral has lain, for three hundred years, the embalmed body of St. Carlo Borromeo. It holds a golden crosier, and has a cross of emeralds on its breast. Admitting the crosier and emeralds to be useful articles, is the body to be considered as "having" them? Do they, in the politico-economical sense of property, belong to it? If not, and if we may, therefore, conclude generally that a dead body cannot possess property, what degree and period of animation in the body will render possession possible?

As thus: lately in a wreck of a Californian ship, one of the passengers fastened a belt about him with two hundred pounds of gold in it, with which he was found afterwards at the bottom. Now, as he was sinking—had he the gold? or had the gold him?

And if, instead of sinking him in the sea by its weight, the gold had struck him on the forehead, and thereby caused incurable disease—suppose palsy or insanity,—would the gold in that case have been more a "possession" than in the first? Without pressing the inquiry up through instances of gradually increasing vital power over the gold (which I will, however, give, if they are asked for), I presume the reader will see that possession, or "having," is not an absolute, but a gradated, power; and consists not only in the quantity or nature of the thing possessed, but also (and in a greater degree) in its suitableness to the person possessing it and in his vital power to use it.

And our definition of Wealth, expanded, becomes: "The possession of useful articles, *which we can use*." This is a very serious change. For wealth, instead of depending merely on a "have," is thus seen to depend on a "can." Gladiator's death, on a "habet"; but soldier's victory, and State's salvation, on a "quo plurimum posset." (Liv. VII. 6.)[6] And what we reasoned of only as accumulation of material, is seen to demand also accumulation of capacity.

63. So much for our verb. Next for our adjective. What is the meaning of "useful"?

The inquiry is closely connected with the last. For what is capable of use in the hands of some persons, is capable, in the hands of others, of the opposite of use, called commonly "from-use," or "ab-use." And it depends on the person, much more than on the article, whether its usefulness or ab-usefulness will be the quality developed in it. Thus, wine, which the Greeks, in their Bacchus, made rightly the type of all passion, and which, when used, "cheereth god and man" [7] (that is to say, strengthens both the divine life, or reasoning power, and the earthy, or carnal power, of man); yet, when abused, becomes "Dionusos," hurtful especially to the divine part of man, or reason. And again, the body itself, being equally liable to use and to abuse, and, when rightly disciplined, serviceable to

[6] A reference to the sacrifice of Marcus Curtius in Livy's *History of Rome*.
[7] Judges 9:13.

the State, both for war and labour;—but when not disciplined, or abused, valueless to the State, and capable only of continuing the private or single existence of the individual (and that but feebly)—the Greeks called such a body an "idiotic" or "private" body, from their word signifying a person employed in no way directly useful to the State; whence finally, our "idiot," meaning a person entirely occupied with his own concerns.

Hence, it follows that if a thing is to be useful, it must be not only of an availing nature, but in availing hands. Or, in accurate terms, usefulness is value in the hands of the valiant; so that this science of wealth being, as we have just seen, when regarded as the science of Accumulation, accumulative of capacity as well as of material,—when regarded as the Science of Distribution, is distribution not absolute, but discriminate; not of every thing to every man, but of the right thing to the right man. A difficult science, dependent on more than arithmetic.

64. Wealth, therefore, is "THE POSSESSION OF THE VALUABLE BY THE VALIANT"; and in considering it as a power existing in a nation, the two elements, the value of the thing, and the valour of its possessor, must be estimated together. Whence it appears that many of the persons commonly considered wealthy, are in reality no more wealthy than the locks of their own strong boxes are, they being inherently and eternally incapable of wealth; and operating for the nation, in an economical point of view, either as pools of dead water, and eddies in a stream (which, so long as the stream flows, are useless, or serve only to drown people, but may become of importance in a state of stagnation should the stream dry); or else,

as dams in a river, of which the ultimate service depends not on the dam, but the miller; or else, as mere accidental stays and impediments, acting not as wealth, but (for we ought to have a correspondent term) as "illth," causing various devastation and trouble around them in all directions; or lastly, act not at all, but are merely animated conditions of delay, (no use being possible of anything they have until they are dead,) in which last condition they are nevertheless often useful *as* delays, and "impedimenta," if a nation is apt to move too fast.

65. This being so, the difficulty of the true science of Political Economy lies not merely in the need of developing manly character to deal with material value, but in the fact, that while the manly character and material value only form wealth by their conjunction, they have nevertheless a mutually destructive operation on each other. For the manly character is apt to ignore, or even cast away, the material value:— whence that of Pope:—

> "Sure, of qualities demanding praise,
>   More go to ruin fortunes, than to raise." [8]

And on the other hand, the material value is apt to undermine the manly character; so that it must be our work, in the issue, to examine what evidence there is of the effect of wealth on the minds of its possessors; also, what kind of person it is who usually sets himself to obtain wealth, and succeeds in doing so; and whether the world owes more gratitude to rich or to poor men, either for their moral indifference upon it, or for chief goods, discoveries, and practical advance-

[8] "Moral Essays," Epistle iii. Ruskin, quoting from memory, makes one small slip.

ments. I may, however, anticipate future conclusions, so far as to state that in a community regulated only by laws of demand and supply, but protected from open violence, the persons who become rich are, generally speaking, industrious, resolute, proud, covetous, prompt, methodical, sensible, unimaginative, insensitive, and ignorant. The persons who remain poor are the entirely foolish, the entirely wise, the idle, the reckless, the humble, the thoughtful, the dull, the imaginative, the sensitive, the well-informed, the improvident, the irregularly and impulsively wicked, the clumsy knave, the open thief, and the entirely merciful, just, and godly person.

66. Thus far, then, of wealth. Next, we have to ascertain the nature of PRICE; that is to say, of exchange value, and its expression by currencies.

Note first, of exchange, there can be no *profit* in it. It is only in labour there can be profit—that is to say, a "making in advance," or "making in favour of" (from proficio). In exchange, there is only advantage, *i.e.*, a bringing of vantage or power to the exchanging persons. Thus, one man, by sowing and reaping, turns one measure of corn into two measures. That is Profit. Another, by digging and forging, turns one spade into two spades. That is Profit. But the man who has two measures of corn wants sometimes to dig; and the man who has two spades wants sometimes to eat:—They exchange the gained grain for the gained tool; and both are the better for the exchange; but though there is much advantage in the transaction, there is no profit. Nothing is constructed or produced. Only that which had been before constructed is given to the person by whom it can be used. If labour is necessary to effect the exchange, that labour is in reality involved in the production, and, like all other labour, bears profit. Whatever number of men are concerned in the manufacture, or in the conveyance, have share in the profit; but neither the manufacture nor the conveyance are the exchange, and in the exchange itself there is no profit.

There may, however, be acquisition, which is a very different thing. If, in the exchange, one man is able to give what cost him little labour for what has cost the other much, he "acquires" a certain quantity of the produce of the other's labour. And precisely what he acquires, the other loses. In mercantile language, the person who thus acquires is commonly said to have "made a profit"; and I believe that many of our merchants are seriously under the impression that it is possible for everybody, somehow, to make a profit in this manner. Whereas, by the unfortunate constitution of the world we live in, the laws both of matter and motion have quite rigorously forbidden universal acquisition of this kind. Profit, or material gain, is attainable only by construction or by discovery; not by exchange. Whenever material gain follows exchange, for every *plus* there is a precisely equal *minus*.

Unhappily for the progress of the science of Political Economy, the plus quantities, or—if I may be allowed to coin an awkward plural—the pluses, make a very positive and venerable appearance in the world, so that every one is eager to learn the science which produces results so magnificent; whereas the minuses have, on the other hand, a tendency to retire into back streets, and other places of shade,—or even to get themselves wholly and finally put out of sight in graves: which renders the algebra of this science peculiar, and difficultly legible; a large number of its negative signs being written by the account-keeper in a kind of red ink, which starvation thins, and makes strangely pale, or even quite invisible ink, for the present.

67. The Science of Exchange, or, as I hear it has been proposed to call it, of "Catallactics," [9] considered as one of gain, is, therefore, simply nugatory; but considered as one of acquisition, it is a very curious science, differing in its data and basis from every other science known. Thus:—If I can exchange a needle with a savage for a diamond, my power of doing so depends either on the savage's ignorance of social arrangements in Europe, or on his want of power to take advantage of them, by selling the diamond to any one else for more needles. If, farther, I make the bargain as completely advantageous to myself as possible, by giving to the savage a needle with no eye in it (reaching, thus a sufficiently satisfactory type of the perfect operation of catallactic science), the advantage to me in the entire transaction depends wholly upon the ignorance, powerlessness, or heedlessness of the person dealt with. Do away with these, and catallactic advantage becomes impossible. So far, therefore, as the science of exchange relates to the advantage of one of the exchanging persons only, it is founded on the ignorance or incapacity of the opposite person. Where these vanish, it also vanishes. It is therefore a science founded on nescience, and an art founded on artlessness. But all other sciences and arts, except this, have for their object the doing away with their opposite nescience and artlessness.

[9] The term is associated with Richard Whately's *Lectures on Political Economy.*

This science, alone of sciences, must, by all available means, promulgate and prolong its opposite nescience; otherwise the science itself is impossible. It is, therefore, peculiarly and alone the science of darkness; probably a bastard science—not by any means a *divina scientia,* but one begotten of another father, that father who, advising his children to turn stones into bread, is himself employed in turning bread into stones, and who, if you ask a fish of him (fish not being producible on his estate), can but give you a serpent.[10]

68. The general law, then, respecting just or economical exchange, is simply this:—There must be advantage on both sides (or if only advantage on one, at least no disadvantage on the other) to the persons exchanging; and just payment for his time, intelligence, and labour, to any intermediate person effecting the transaction (commonly called a merchant); and whatever advantage there is on either side, and whatever pay is given to the intermediate person, should be thoroughly known to all concerned. All attempt at concealment implies some practice of the opposite, or undivine science, founded on nescience. Whence another saying of the Jew merchant's—"As a nail between the stone joints, so doth sin stick fast between buying and selling."[11] Which peculiar riveting of stone and timber, in men's dealings with each other, is again set forth in the house which was to be destroyed—timber and stones together—when Zechariah's roll (more probably "curved sword")[12] flew

[10] Cf. Matthew 7:10.
[11] Ecclesiasticus 27:2.
[12] Cf. Zechariah 5:1-2. The rest of the quotations in this passage derive from Zechariah 5.

over it: "the curse that goeth forth over all the earth upon every one that stealeth and holdeth himself guiltless," instantly followed by the vision of the Great Measure;—the measure "of the injustice of them in all the earth" (αὕτη ἡ ἀδικία αὐτῶν ἐν πά σῃ τῇ γῇ), with the weight of lead for its lid, and the woman, the spirit of wickedness, within it;—that is to say, Wickedness hidden by dulness, and formalized, outwardly, into ponderously established cruelty. "It shall be set upon its own base in the land of Babel."

69. I have hitherto carefully restricted myself, in speaking of exchange, to the use of the term "advantage"; but that term includes two ideas: the advantage, namely, of getting what we *need*, and that of getting what we *wish for*. Three-fourths of the demands existing in the world are romantic; founded on visions, idealisms, hopes, and affections; and the regulation of of the purse is, in its essence, regulation of the imagination and the heart. Hence, the right discussion of the nature of price is a very high metaphysical and psychical problem; sometimes to be solved only in a passionate manner, as by David in his counting the price of the water of the well by the gate of Bethlehem;[13] but its first conditions are the following:—The price of anything is the quantity of labour given by the person desiring it, in order to obtain possession of it. This price depends on four variable quantities. A. The quantity of wish the purchaser has for the thing; opposed to *a*, the quantity of wish the seller has to keep it. B. The quantity of labour the purchaser can afford, to obtain the thing; opposed to *β*, the quantity of labour the seller can afford to keep it. These

[13] Cf. II Samuel 23:15-16

quantities are operative only in excess; *i.e.*, the quantity of wish (A) means the quantity of wish for this thing, above wish for other things; and the quantity of work (B) means the quantity which can be spared to get this thing from the quantity needed to get other things.

Phenomena of price, therefore, are intensely complex, curious, and interesting—too complex, however, to be examined yet; every one of them, when traced far enough, showing itself at last as a part of the bargain of the Poor of the Flock (or "flock of slaughter"),[14] "If ye think good, give ME my price, and if not, forbear"—Zech. xi. 12; but as the price of everything is to be calculated finally in labour, it is necessary to define the nature of that standard.

70. Labour is the contest of the life of man with and opposite;—the term "life" including his intellect, soul, and physical power, contending with question, difficulty, trial, or material force.

Labour is of a higher or lower order, as it includes more or fewer of the elements of life: and labour of good quality, in any kind, includes always as much intellect and feeling as will fully and harmoniously regulate the physical force.

In speaking of the value and price of labour, it is necessary always to understand labour of a given rank and quality, as we should speak of gold or silver of a given standard. Bad (that is, heartless, inexperienced, or senseless) labour cannot be valued; it is like gold of uncertain alloy, or flawed iron.

The quality and kind of labour being given, its value, like that of all other valuable things, is in-

[14] Zechariah 11:7.

variable. But the quantity of it which must be given for other things is variable: and in estimating this variation, the price of other things must always be counted by the quantity of labour; not the price of labour by the quantity of other things.

71. Thus, if we want to plant an apple sapling in rocky ground, it may take two hours' work; in soft ground, perhaps only half an hour. Grant the soil equally good for the tree in each case. Then the value of the sapling planted by two hours' work is nowise greater than that of the sapling planted in half an hour. One will bear no more fruit than the other. Also, one half-hour of work is as valuable as another half-hour; nevertheless, the one sapling has cost four such pieces of work, the other only one. Now, the proper statement of this fact is, not that the labour on the hard ground is cheaper than on the soft; but that the tree is dearer. The exchange value may, or may not, afterwards depend on this fact. If other people have plenty of soft ground to plant in, they will take no cognizance of our two hours' labour in the price they will offer for the plant on the rock. And if, through want of sufficient botanical science, we have planted an upas-tree instead of an apple, the exchange value will be a negative quantity; still less proportionate to the labour expended.

What is commonly called cheapness of labour, signifies, therefore, in reality, that many obstacles have to be overcome by it; so that much labour is required to produce a small result. But this should never be spoken of as cheapness of labour, but as dearness of the object wrought for. It would be just as rational to say that walking was cheap, because we had ten miles to walk home to our dinner, as that labour was cheap, because we had to work ten hours to earn it.

72. The last word which we have to define is "Production."

I have hitherto spoken of all labour as profitable; because it is impossible to consider under one head the quality or value of labour, and its aim. But labour of the best quality may be various in aim. It may be either constructive ("gathering," from con and struo), as agriculture; nugatory, as jewel-cutting; or destructive ("scattering," from de and struo), as war. It is not, however, always easy to prove labour, apparently nugatory, to be actually so; generally, the formula holds good: "he that gathereth not, scattereth";[15] thus, the jeweller's art is probably very harmful in its ministering to a clumsy and inelegant pride. So that, finally, I believe nearly all labour may be shortly divided into positive and negative labour: positive, that which produces life; negative, that which produces death; the most directly negative labour being murder, and the most directly positive, the bearing and rearing of children: so that in the precise degree in which murder is hateful, on the negative side of idleness, in that exact degree child-rearing is admirable, on the positive side of idleness. For which reason, and because of the honour that there is in rearing children, while the wife is said to be as the vine (for cheering), the children are as the olive branch,[16] for praise: nor for praise only, but for peace (because large families can only be reared in times of peace): though since, in their spreading and voyaging

[15] Cf. Matthew 12:30.
[16] Cf. Psalms 128:3.

in various directions, they distribute strength, they are, to the home strength, as arrows in the hand of the giant[17]—striking here and there far away.

Labour being thus various in its result, the prosperity of any nation is in exact proportion to the quantity of labour which it spends in obtaining and employing means of life. Observe,—I say, obtaining and employing; that is to say, not merely wisely producing, but wisely distributing and consuming. Economists usually speak as if there were no good in consumption absolute. So far from this being so, consumption absolute is the end, crown, and perfection of production; and wise consumption is a far more difficult art than wise production. Twenty people can gain money for one who can use it; and the vital question, for individual and for nation, is, never "how much do they make?" but "to what purpose do they spend?"

73. The reader may, perhaps, have been surprised at the slight reference I have hitherto made to "capital," and its functions. It is here the place to define them.

Capital signifies "head, or source, or root material"— it is material by which some derivative or secondary good is produced. It is only capital proper (caput vivum, not caput mortuum) when it is thus producing something different from itself. It is a root, which does not enter into vital function till it produces something else than a root: namely, fruit. That fruit will in time again produce roots; and so all living capital issues in reproduction of capital; but capital which produces nothing but capital is only root producing root; bulb issuing in bulb, never in tulip; seed issuing in seed, never in bread. The Political Economy of Europe has

[17] Cf. Psalms 127:4.

hitherto devoted itself wholly to the multiplication, or
(less even) the aggregation, of bulbs. It never saw,
nor conceived, such a thing as a tulip. Nay, boiled
bulbs they might have been—glass bulbs—Prince
Rupert's drops,[18] consummated in powder (well, if
it were glass-powder and not gunpower), for any
end or meaning the economists had in defining the
laws of aggregation. We will try and get a clearer
notion of them.

The best and simplest general type of capital is
a well-made ploughshare. Now, if that ploughshare
did nothing but beget other ploughshares, in a polypous manner,—however the great cluster of polypous
plough might glitter in the sun, it would have lost its
function of capital. It becomes true capital only by
another kind of splendour,—when it is seen "splendes-
cere sulco," [19] to grow bright in the furrow; rather
with diminution of its substance, than addition, by
the noble friction. And the true home question, to
every capitalist and to every nation, is not, "how many
ploughs have you?" but, "where are your furrows?"
not—"how quickly will this capital reproduce itself?"—but, "what will it do during reproduction?"
What substance will it furnish, good for life? what
work construct, protective of life? if none, its own
reproduction is useless—if worse than none,—(for
capital may destroy life as well as support it), its own
reproduction is worse than useless; it is merely an
advance from Tisiphone,[20] on mortgage—not a profit
by any means.

74. Not a profit, as the ancients truly saw, and

[18] A child's toy.
[19] Cf. Virgil, *Georgics*, i, 46.
[20] One of the Eumenides.

showed in the type of Ixion;—for capital is the head, or fountain head, of wealth—the "well-head" of wealth, as the clouds are the well-heads of rain: but when clouds are without water,[21] and only beget clouds, they issue in wrath at last, instead of rain, and in lightning instead of harvest; whence Ixion is said first to have invited his guests to a banquet, and then made them fall into a pit filled with fire; which is the type of the temptation of riches issuing in imprisoned torment,—torment in a pit, (as also Demas' silver mine,)[22] after which, to show the rage of riches passing from lust of pleasure to lust of power, yet power not truly understood, Ixion is said to have desired Juno, and instead, embracing a cloud (or phantasm), to have begotten the Centaurs; the power of mere wealth being, in itself, as the embrace of a shadow,—comfortless, (so also "Ephraim feedeth on wind and followeth after the east wind";[23] or "that which is not"—Prov. xxiii, 5; and again Dante's Geryon,[24] the type of avaricious fraud, as he flies, gathers the *air* up with retractile claws,—"l'aer a se raccolse,") but in its offspring, a mingling of the brutal with the human nature: human in sagacity—using both intellect and arrow; but brutal in its body and hoof, for consuming, and trampling down. For which sin Ixion is at last bound upon a wheel—fiery and toothed, and rolling perpetually in the air;—the type of human labour when selfish and fruitless (kept far into the Middle Ages in their wheel of fortune); the wheel which has in it no breath or spirit, but is whirled by chance only; whereas of all

[21] Cf. Jude, verse 12.
[22] Cf. *The Pilgrim's Progress*, Part I.
[23] Hosea 12:1.
[24] Inferno, Canto 17, 1. 105.

true work the Ezekiel vision is true, that the Spirit of the living creature is in the wheels, and where the angels go, the wheels go by them;[25] but move no otherwise.

75. This being the real nature of capital, it follows that there are two kinds of true production, always going on in an active State: one of seed, and one of food; or production for the Ground, and for the Mouth; both of which are by covetous persons thought to be production only for the granary; whereas the function of the granary is but intermediate and conservative, fulfilled in distribution; else it ends in nothing but mildew, and nourishment of rats and worms. And since production for the Ground is only useful with future hope of harvest, all *essential* production is for the Mouth; and is finally measured by the mouth; hence, as I said above, consumption is the crown of production; and the wealth of a nation is only to be estimated by what it consumes.

The want of any clear sight of this fact is the capital error, issuing in rich interest and revenue of error among the political economists. Their minds are continually set on money-gain, not on mouth-gain; and they fall into every sort of net and snare, dazzled by the coin-glitter as birds by the fowler's glass; or rather (for there is not much else like birds in them) they are like children trying to jump on the heads of their own shadows; the money-gain being only the shadow of the true gain, which is humanity.

76. The final object of political economy, therefore, is to get good method of consumption, and great quantity of consumption: in other words, to use everything, and to use it nobly; whether it be substance,

[25] Ezekiel 1:15f.

service, or service perfecting substance. The most
curious error in Mr. Mill's entire work, (provided
for him originally by Ricardo,) is his endeavour to
distinguish between direct and indirect service, and
consequent assertion that a demand for commodities
is not demand for labour (I. v. 9, *et seq.*). He dis-
tinguishes between labourers employed to lay out
pleasure grounds, and to manufacture velvet; declaring
that it makes material difference to the labouring
classes in which of these two ways a capitalist spends
his money; because the employment of the gardeners
is a demand for labour, but the purchase of velvet is
not. Error colossal, as well as strange. It will, indeed,
make a difference to the labourer whether we bid
him swing his scythe in the spring winds, or drive
the loom in pestilential air; but, so far as his pocket
is concerned, it makes to him absolutely no difference
whether we order him to make green velvet, with seed
and a scythe, or red velvet, with silk and scissors. Neither does it anywise concern him whether, when the
velvet is made, we consume it by walking on it, or
wearing it, so long as our consumption of it is wholly
selfish. But if our consumption is to be in anywise unselfish, not only our mode of consuming the articles we
require interests him, but also the *kind* of article we
require with a view to consumption. As thus (return-
ing for a moment to Mr. Mill's great hardware theory)
it matters, so far as the labourer's immediate profit is
concerned, not an iron filing whether I employ him in
growing a peach, or forging a bombshell; but my
probable mode of consumption of those articles matters
seriously. Admit that it is to be in both cases "unselfish," and the difference, to him, is final, whether when
his child is ill, I walk into his cottage and give it the

peach, or drop the shell down his chimney, and blow his roof off.

The worst of it, for the peasant, is, that the capitalist's consumption of the peach is apt to be selfish, and of the shell, distributive; but, in all cases, this is the broad and general fact, that on due catallactic commercial principles, *somebody's* roof must go off in fulfilment of the bomb's destiny. You may grow for your neighbour, at your liking, grapes, or grape-shot; he will also, catallactically, grow grapes or grape-shot for you, and you will each reap what you have sown.[26]

77. It is, therefore, the manner and issue of consumption which are the real tests of production. Production does not consist in things laboriously made, but in things serviceably consumable; and the question for the nation is not how much labour it employs, but how much life it produces. For as consumption is the end and aim of production, so life is the end and aim of consumption.

I left this question to the reader's thought two months ago, choosing rather that he should work it out for himself than have it sharply stated to him. But now, the ground being sufficiently broken (and the details into which the several questions, here opened, must lead us, being too complex for discussion in the pages of a periodical, so that I must pursue them elsewhere), I desire, in closing the series of introductory papers, to leave this one great fact clearly stated. THERE IS NO WEALTH BUT LIFE. Life, including all its powers of love, of joy, and of admiration. That country is the richest which nourishes the greatest number of noble and happy human beings; that man is richest who, having perfected the functions of his own life to

[26] Cf. Galatians 6:7.

the utmost, has also the widest helpful influence, both personal, and by means of his possessions, over the lives of others.

A strange political economy; the only one, nevertheless, that ever was or can be: all political economy founded on self-interest being but the fulfilment of that which once brought schism into the Policy of angels, and ruin into the Economy of Heaven.

78. "The greatest number of human beings noble and happy." But is the nobleness consistent with the number? Yes, not only consistent with it, but essential to it. The maximum of life can only be reached by the maximum of virtue. In this respect the law of human population differs wholly from that of animal life. The multiplication of animals is checked only by want of food, and by the hostility of races; the population of the gnat is restrained by the hunger of the swallow, and that of the swallow by the scarcity of gnats. Man, considered as an animal, is indeed limited by the same laws: hunger, or plague, or war, are the necessary and only restraints upon his increase,—effectual restraints hitherto,—his principal study having been how most swiftly to destroy himself, or ravage his dwelling-places, and his highest skill directed to give range to the famine, seed to the plague, and sway to the sword. But, considered as other than an animal, his increase is not limited by these laws. It is limited only by the limits of his courage and his love. Both of these *have* their bounds; and ought to have; his race has its bounds also; but these have not yet been reached, nor will be reached for ages.

79. In all the ranges of human thought I know none so melancholy as the speculations of political economists on the population question. It is proposed to

better the condition of the labourer by giving him higher wages. "Nay," says the economist,—"if you raise his wages, he will either people down to the same point of misery at which you found him, or drink your wages away." He will. I know it. Who gave him this will? Suppose it were your own son of whom you spoke, declaring to me that you dared not take him into your firm, nor even give him his just labourer's wages, because if you did he would die of drunkenness, and leave half a score of children to the parish. "Who gave your son these dispositions?"—I should enquire. Has he them by inheritance or by education? By one or other they *must* come; and as in him, so also in the poor. Either these poor are of a race essentially different from ours, and unredeemable (which, however often implied, I have heard none yet openly say), or else by such care as we have ourselves received, we may make them continent and sober as ourselves— wise and dispassionate as we are—models arduous of imitation. "But," it is answered, "they cannot receive education." Why not? That is precisely the point at issue. Charitable persons suppose the worst fault of the rich is to refuse the people meat; and the people cry for their meat, kept back by fraud, to the Lord of Multitudes.[27] Alas! it is not meat of which the refusal is cruelest, or to which the claim is validest. The life is more than the meat.[28] The rich not only refuse food to the poor; they refuse wisdom; they refuse virtue; they refuse salvation. Ye sheep without shepherd,[29] it is not the pasture that has been shut from you, but the Presence. Meat! perhaps your right to that may be

[27] James 5:4.
[28] Cf. Matthew 6:25.
[29] *Ibid.*, 9:36.

pleadable; but other rights have to be pleaded first. Claim your crumbs from the table if you will; but claim them as children, not as dogs; claim your right to be fed, but claim more loudly your right to be holy, perfect, and pure.

Strange words to be used of working people! "What! holy; without any long robes or anointing oils; these rough-jacketed, rough-worded persons; set to nameless, dishonoured service? Perfect!—these, with dim eyes and cramped limbs, and slowly wakening minds? Pure!—these, with sensual desire and grovelling thought; foul of body and coarse of soul?" It may be so; nevertheless, such as they are, they are the holiest, perfectest, purest persons the earth can at present show. They may be what you have said; but if so, they yet are holier than we who have left them thus.

But what can be done for them? Who can clothe— who teach—who restrain their multitudes? What end can there be for them at last, but to consume one another?

I hope for another end, though not, indeed, from any of the three remedies for over-population commonly suggested by economists.

80. These three are, in brief—Colonization; Bringing in of waste lands; or Discouragement of Marriage.

The first and second of these expedients merely evade or delay the question. It will, indeed, be long before the world has been all colonized, and its deserts all brought under cultivation. But the radical question is, not how much habitable land is in the world, but how many human beings ought to be maintained on a given space of habitable land.

Observe, I say, *ought* to be, not how many *can* be. Ricardo, with his usual inaccuracy, defines what he calls the "natural rate of wages" as "that which will maintain the labourer." Maintain him! yes; but how? —the question was instantly thus asked of me by a working girl, to whom I read the passage. I will amplify her question for her. "Maintain him, how?" As, first, to what length of life? Out of a given number of fed persons, how many are to be old—how many young? that is to say, will you arrange their maintenance so as to kill them early—say at thirty or thirty-five on the average, including deaths of weakly or ill-fed children?—or so as to enable them to live out a natural life? You will feed a greater number, in the first case, by rapidity of succession; probably a happier number in the second: which does Mr. Ricardo mean to be their natural state, and to which state belongs the natural rate of wages?

Again: A piece of land which will only support ten idle, ignorant, and improvident persons, will support thirty or forty intelligent and industrious ones. Which of these is their natural state, and to which of them belongs the natural rate of wages?

Again: If a piece of land support forty persons in industrious ignorance; and if, tired of this ignorance, they set apart ten of their number to study the properties of cones, and the sizes of stars; the labour of these ten being withdrawn from the ground, must either tend to the increase of food in some transitional manner, or the persons set apart for sidereal and conic purposes must starve, or some one else starve instead of them. What is, therefore, the natural rate of wages of the scientific persons, and how does this rate relate to, or measure, their reverted or transitional productiveness?

Again: If the ground maintains, at first, forty labourers in a peaceable and pious state of mind, but they become in a few years so quarrelsome and impious that they have to set apart five, to meditate upon and settle their disputes;—ten, armed to the teeth with costly instruments, to enforce the decisions; and five to remind everybody in an eloquent manner of the existence of a God;—what will be the result upon the general power of production, and what is the "natural rate of wages" of the meditative, muscular, and oracular labourers?

81. Leaving these questions to be discussed, or waived, at their pleasure, by Mr. Ricardo's followers, I proceed to state the main facts bearing on that probable future of the labouring classes which has been partially glanced at by Mr. Mill. That chapter and the preceding one[30] differ from the common writing of political economists in admitting some value in the aspect of nature, and expressing regret at the probability of the destruction of natural scenery. But we may spare our anxieties on this head. Men can neither drink steam, nor eat stone. The maximum of population on a given space of land implies also the relative maximum of edible vegetable, whether for men or cattle; it implies a maximum of pure air, and of pure water. Therefore: a maximum of wood, to transmute the air, and of sloping ground, protected by herbage from the extreme heat of the sun, to feed the streams. All England may, if it so chooses, become one manufacturing town; and Englishmen, sacrificing themselves to the good of general humanity, may live diminished lives in the midst of noise, of darkness, and of deadly exhalation. But the world cannot become a factory nor a mine. No amount of ingenuity will ever

[30] Cf. *Principles of Political Economy* Book IV, chs. vi, vii.

make iron digestible by the million, nor substitute hydrogen for wine. Neither the avarice nor the rage of men will ever feed them; and however the apple of Sodom and the grape of Gomorrah may spread their table for a time with dainties of ashes, and nectar of asps,—so long as men live by bread, the far away valleys must laugh as they are covered with the gold of God, and the shouts of His happy multitudes ring round the winepress and the well.

82. Nor need our more sentimental economists fear the too wide spread of the formalities of a mechanical agriculture. The presence of a wise population implies the search for felicity as well as for food; nor can any population reach its maximum but through that wisdom which "rejoices" in the habitable parts of the earth.[31] The desert has its appointed place and work; the eternal engine, whose beam is the earth's axle, whose beat is its year, and whose breath is its ocean, will still divide imperiously to their desert kingdoms bound with unfurrowable rock, and swept by unarrested sand, their powers of frost and fire: but the zones and lands between, habitable, will be loveliest in habitation. The desire of the heart is also the light of the eyes.[32] No scene is continually and untiringly loved, but one rich by joyful human labour; smooth in field; fair in garden; full in orchard; trim, sweet, and frequent in homestead; ringing with voices of vivid existence. No air is sweet that is silent; it is only sweet when full of low currents of under sound— triplets of birds, and murmur and chirp of insects, and deep-toned words of men, and wayward trebles of childhood. As the art of life is learned, it will be

[31] Cf. Proverbs 8:31.
[32] *Ibid.*, 15:30.

found at last that all lovely things are also necessary;—
the wild flower by the wayside, as well as the tended
corn; and the wild birds and creatures of the forest, as
well as the tended cattle; because man doth not live
by bread only,[33] but also by the desert manna; by
every wondrous word and unknowable work of God.
Happy, in that he knew them not, nor did his fathers
know; and that round about him reaches yet into the
infinite, the amazement of his existence.

83. Note, finally, that all effectual advancement towards this true felicity of the human race must be
by individual, not public effort. Certain general measures may aid, certain revised laws guide, such advancement; but the measure and law which have first
to be determined are those of each man's home. We
continually hear it recommended by sagacious people to complaining neighbours (usually less well
placed in the world than themselves), that they should
"remain content in the station in which Providence
has placed them." There are perhaps some circumstances of life in which Providence has no intention
that people *should* be content. Nevertheless, the
maxim is on the whole a good one; but it is peculiarly
for home use. That your neighbour should, or should
not, remain content with *his* position, is not your
business; but it is very much your business to remain
content with your own. What is chiefly needed in
England at the present day is to show the quantity
of pleasure that may be obtained by a consistent, well-
administered competence, modest, confessed, and la-
borious. We need examples of people who, leaving
Heaven to decide whether they are to rise in the
world, decide for themselves that they will be happy

[33] Deuteronomy 8:3 and elsewhere in the Bible.

in it, and have resolved to seek—not greater wealth,
but simpler pleasure; not higher fortune, but deeper
felicity; making the first of possessions, self-possession;
and honouring themselves in the harmless pride and
calm pursuits of peace.

Of which lowly peace it is written that "justice and
peace have kissed each other"; and that the fruit of
justice is "sown in peace of them that make peace";[34]
not "peace-makers" in the common understanding—
reconcilers of quarrels; (though that function also follows on the greater one;) but peace-Creators; Givers
of Calm. Which you cannot give, unless you first gain;
nor is this gain one which will follow assuredly on
any course of business, commonly so called. No form
of gain is less probable, business being (as is shown
in the language of all nations—πωλεῖν from πέλω, πρᾶρις
from περάω, venire, vendre, and venal, from venio,
etc.) essentially restless—and probably contentious;—
having a raven-like mind to the motion to and fro, as
to the carrion food; whereas the olive-feeding and
bearing birds look for rest for their feet;[35] thus it is
said of Wisdom that she "hath builded her house,
and hewn out her seven pillars";[36] and even when,
though apt to wait long at the doorposts, she has to
leave her house and go abroad, her paths are peace[37]
also.

84. For us, at all events, her work must begin at
the entry of the doors: all true economy is "Law of the
house." Strive to make that law strict, simple, gener-
ous: waste nothing, and grudge nothing. Care in no-

[34] Cf. Psalms 85:10.
[35] Cf. Genesis 8:9.
[36] Proverbs 9:1.
[37] *Ibid.*, 3:17.

wise to make more of money, but care to make much of it; remembering always the great, palpable, inevitable fact—the rule and root of all economy—that what one person has, another cannot have; and that every atom of substance, of whatever kind, used or consumed, is so much human life spent; which, if it issue in the saving present life, or gaining more, is well spent, but if not is either so much life prevented, or so much slain. In all buying, consider, first, what condition of existence you cause in the producers of what you buy; secondly, whether the sum you have paid is just to the producer, and in due proportion, lodged in his hands; thirdly, to how much clear use, for food, knowledge, or joy, this that you have bought can be put; and fourthly, to whom and in what way it can be most speedily and serviceably distributed; in all dealings whatsoever insisting on entire openness and stern fulfilment; and in all doings on perfection and loveliness of accomplishment; especially on fineness and purity of all marketable commodity: watching at the same time for all ways of gaining, or teaching, powers of simple pleasure; and of showing "ὅσον ἐν ἀσφοδέλῳ μέγ ὄνειαρ" [38]—the sum of enjoyment depending not on the quantity of things tasted, but on the vivacity and patience of taste.

85. And if, on due and honest thought over these things, it seems that the kind of existence to which men are now summoned by every plea of pity and claim of right, may, for some time at least, not be a luxurious one;—consider whether, even supposing it guiltless, luxury would be desired by any of us, if we saw clearly at our sides the suffering which accompanies it in the world. Luxury is indeed possible in the

[38] Cf. Hesiod, *Works and Days,* 11. 40-1.

future—innocent and exquisite; luxury for all, and by the help of all; but luxury at present can only be enjoyed by the ignorant; the cruelest man living could not sit at his feast, unless he sat blindfold. Raise the veil boldly; face the light, and if, as yet, the light of the eye can only be through tears, and the light of the body[39] through sackcloth, go thou forth weeping, bearing precious seed, until the time come, and the kingdom, when Christ's gift of bread, and bequest of peace, shall be "Unto this last as unto thee";[40] and when, for earth's severed multitudes of the wicked and the weary, there shall be holier reconciliation than that of the narrow home, and calm economy, where the Wicked cease—not from trouble, but from troubling—and the Weary are at rest.[41]

[39] Cf. Matthew 6:22.
[40] *Ibid.*, 20:14.
[41] Cf. Job 3:17.

TRAFFIC

Delivered in the Town Hall, Bradford
April 21, 1864

1. My good Yorkshire friends, you asked me down here among your hills that I might talk to you about this Exchange you are going to build: but, earnestly and seriously asking you to pardon me, I am going to do nothing of the kind. I cannot talk, or at least can say very little, about this same Exchange. I must talk of quite other things, though not willingly;—I could not deserve your pardon, if, when you invited me to speak on one subject, I *wilfully* [*sic.*] spoke on another. But I cannot speak, to purpose, of anything about which I do not care; and most simply and sorrowfully I have to tell you, in the outset, that I do *not* care about this Exchange of yours.

2. If, however, when you sent me your invitation, I had answered, "I won't come, I don't care about the Exchange of Bradford," you would have been justly offended with me, not knowing the reasons of so blunt a carelessness. So I have come down, hoping that you will patiently let me tell you why, on this, and many other such occasions, I now remain silent, when formerly I should have caught at the opportunity of speaking to a gracious audience.

3. In a word, then, I do not care about this Exchange—because *you* don't; and because you know

perfectly well I cannot make you. Look at the essential
conditions of the case, which you, as business men,
know perfectly well, though perhaps you think I
forget them. You are going to spend £30,000, which
to you, collectively, is nothing; the buying a new coat
is, as to the cost of it, a much more important matter
of consideration to me, than building a new Exchange
is to you. But you think you may as well have the
right thing for your money. You know there are a
great many odd styles of architecture about; you don't
want to do anything ridiculous; you hear of me, among
others, as a respectable architectural man-milliner;
and you send for me, that I may tell you the leading
fashion; and what is, in our shops, for the moment,
the newest and sweetest thing in pinnacles.

4. Now, pardon me for telling you frankly, you
cannot have good architecture merely by asking people's advice on occasion. All good architecture is the
expression of national life and character; and it is
produced by a prevalent and eager national taste, or
desire for beauty. And I want you to think a little of
the deep significance of this word "taste"; for no statement of mine has been more earnestly or oftener
controverted than that good taste is essentially a
moral quality. "No," say many of my antagonists,
"taste is one thing, morality is another. Tell us what
is pretty: we shall be glad to know that; but we need
no sermons—even were you able to preach them,
which may be doubted."

5. Permit me, therefore, to fortify this old dogma of
mine somewhat. Taste is not only a part and an index
of morality;—it is the ONLY morality. The first, and
last, and closest trial question to any living creature is,
"What do you like?" Tell me what you like, and I'll

tell you what you are. Go out into the street, and ask
the first man or woman you meet, what their "taste"
is; and if they answer candidly, you know them, body
and soul. "You, my friend in the rags, with the un-
steady gait, what do *you* like?" "A pipe, and a quartern
of gin." I know you. "You, good woman, with the quick
step and tidy bonnet, what do you like?" "A swept
hearth, and a clean tea-table; and my husband opposite me, and a baby at my breast." Good, I know
you also. "You, little girl with the golden hair and the
soft eyes, what do you like?" "My canary, and a run
among the wood hyacinths." "You, little boy with the
dirty hands, and the low forehead, what do you like?"
"A shy at the sparrows, and a game at pitch farthing."
Good; we know them all now. What more need we
ask?

6. "Nay," perhaps you answer; "we need rather to
ask what these people and children do, than what
they like. If they *do* right, it is no matter that they like
what is wrong; and if they *do* wrong, it is no matter
that they like what is right. Doing is the great thing;
and it does not matter that the man likes drinking, so
that he does not drink; nor that the little girl likes to
be kind to her canary, if she will not learn her lessons;
nor that the little boy likes throwing stones at the
sparrows, if he goes to the Sunday school." Indeed,
for a short time, and in a provisional sense, this is true.
For if, resolutely, people do what is right, in time to
come they like doing it. But they only are in a right
moral state when they *have* come to like doing it; and
as long as they don't like it, they are still in a vicious
state. The man is not in health of body who is always
thinking of the bottle in the cupboard, though he
bravely bears his thirst; but the man who heartily en-

joys water in the morning, and wine in the evening, each in its proper quantity and time. And the entire object of true education is to make people not merely *do* the right things, but *enjoy* the right things:—not merely industrious, but to love industry—not merely learned, but to love knowledge—not merely pure, but to love purity—not merely just, but to hunger and thirst after justice.[1]

7. But you may answer or think, "Is the liking for outside ornaments,—for pictures, or statues, or furniture, or architecture, a moral quality?" Yes, most surely, if a rightly set liking. Taste for *any* pictures or statues is not a moral quality, but taste for good ones is. Only here again we have to define the word "good." I don't mean by "good," clever—or learned—or difficult in the doing. Take a picture by Teniers,[2] of sots quarrelling over their dice; it is an entirely clever picture; so clever that nothing in its kind has ever been done equal to it; but it is also an entirely base and evil picture. It is an expression of delight in the prolonged contemplation of a vile thing, and delight in that is an "unmannered," or "immoral" quality. It is "bad taste" in the profoundest sense—it is the taste of the devils. On the other hand, a picture of Titian's, or a Greek statue, or a Greek coin, or a Turner landscape, expresses delight in the perpetual contemplation of a good and perfect thing. That is an entirely moral quality—it is the taste of the angels. And all delight in fine art, and all love of it, resolve themselves into simple love of that which deserves love.

[1] Cf. Matthew 5:6.
[2] David Teniers the younger (1610-1690), known for his realistic studies of rural life. While sometimes—with reluctance—recognizing Teniers's technique, Ruskin is generally critical of this artist.

That deserving is the quality which we call "loveliness"—(we ought to have an opposite word, hateliness, to be said of the things which deserve to be hated); and it is not an indifferent nor optional thing whether we love this or that; but it is just the vital function of all our being. What we *like* determines what we *are*, and is the sign of what we are; and to teach taste is inevitably to form character.

8. As I was thinking over this, in walking up Fleet Street the other day, my eye caught the title of a book standing open in a bookseller's window. It was —"On the necessity of the diffusion of taste among all classes." "Ah," I thought to myself, "my classifying friend, when you have diffused your taste, where will your classes be? The man who likes what you like, belongs to the same class with you, I think. Inevitably so. You may put him to other work if you choose; but, by the condition you have brought him into, he will dislike the work as much as you would yourself. You get hold of a scavenger or a costermonger, who enjoyed the Newgate Calendar for literature, and 'Pop goes the Weasel' for music. You think you can make him like Dante and Beethoven? I wish you joy of your lessons; but if you do, you have made a gentleman of him:—he won't like to go back to his costermongering."

9. And so completely and unexceptionally is this so, that, if I had time to-night, I could show you that a nation cannot be affected by any vice, or weakness, without expressing it, legibly, and for ever, either in bad art, or by want of art; and that there is no national virtue, small or great, which is not manifestly expressed in all the art which circumstances enable the people possessing that virtue to produce. Take, for

instance, your great English virtue of enduring and patient courage. You have at present in England only one art of any consequence—that is, iron-working. You know thoroughly well how to cast and hammer iron. Now, do you think, in those masses of lava which you build volcanic cones to melt, and which you forge at the mouths of the Infernos you have created; do you think, on those iron plates, your courage and endurance are not written for ever,—not merely with an iron pen, but on iron parchment? And take also your great English vice—European vice—vice of all the world—vice of all other worlds that roll or shine in heaven, bearing with them yet the atmosphere of hell—the vice of jealousy, which brings competition into your commerce, treachery into your councils, and dishonour into your wars—that vice which has rendered for you, and for your next neighbouring nation, the daily occupations of existence no longer possible, but with the mail upon your breasts and the sword loose in its sheath; so that at last, you have realised for all the multitudes of the two great peoples who lead the so-called civilization of the earth,—you have realised for them all, I say, in person and in policy, what was once true only of the rough Border riders of your Cheviot hills—

> "They carved at the meal
> With gloves of steel,
> And they drank the red wine through the helmet
> barr'd;" [3]—

do you think that this national shame and dastardliness of heart are not written as legibly on every rivet of your iron armour as the strength of the right hands that forged it?

[3] Scott, *The Lay of the Last Minstrel,* Canto i, stanza 4.

10. Friends, I know not whether this thing be the more ludicrous or the more melancholy. It is quite unspeakably both. Suppose, instead of being now sent for by you, I had been sent for by some private gentleman, living in a suburban house, with his garden separated only by a fruit wall from his next door neighbour's; and he had called me to consult with him on the furnishing of his drawing-room. I begin looking about me, and find the walls rather bare; I think such and such a paper might be desirable—perhaps a little fresco here and there on the ceiling—a damask curtain or so at the windows. "Ah," says my employer, "damask curtains, indeed! That's all very fine, but you know I can't afford that kind of thing just now!" "Yet the world credits you with a splendid income!" "Ah, yes," says my friend, "but do you know, at present I am obliged to spend it nearly all in steel-traps?" "Steel-traps! for whom?" "Why, for that fellow on the other side the wall, you know: we're very good friends, capital friends; but we are obliged to keep our traps set on both sides of the wall; we could not possibly keep on friendly terms without them, and our spring guns. The worst of it is, we are both clever fellows enough; and there's never a day passes that we won't find out a new trap, or a new gun-barrel, or something; we spend about fifteen millions a year each in our traps, take it altogether; and I don't see how we're to do with less." A highly comic state of life for two private gentlemen! but for two nations, it seems to me, not wholly comic. Bedlam would be comic, perhaps, if there were only one madman in it; and your Christmas pantomime is comic, when there is only one clown in it; but when the whole world turns clown, and paints itself red with its own heart's blood

instead of vermilion, it is something else than comic, I think.

11. Mind, I know a great deal of this is play, and willingly allow for that. You don't know what to do with yourselves for a sensation: fox-hunting and cricketing will not carry you through the whole of this unendurably long mortal life: you liked pop-guns when you were schoolboys, and rifles and Armstrongs are only the same things better made: but then the worst of it is, that what was play to you when boys, was not play to the sparrows; and what is play to you now, is not play to the small birds of State neither; and for the black eagles, you are somewhat shy of taking shots at them, if I mistake not.

12. I must get back to the matter in hand, however. Believe me, without farther instance, I could show you, in all time, that every nation's vice, or virtue, was written in its art: the soldiership of early Greece; the sensuality of late Italy; the visionary religion of Tuscany; the splendid human energy of Venice. I have no time to do this to-night (I have done it elsewhere before now); but I proceed to apply the principle to ourselves in a more searching manner.

13. I notice that among all the new buildings which cover your once wild hills, churches and schools are mixed in due, that is to say, in large proportion, with your mills and mansions; and I notice also that the churches and schools are almost always Gothic, and the mansions and mills are never Gothic. May I ask the meaning of this? for, remember, it is peculiarly a modern phenomenon. When Gothic was invented, houses were Gothic as well as churches; and when the Italian style superseded the Gothic, churches were Italian as well as houses. If there is a Gothic spire to

the cathedral of Antwerp, there is a Gothic belfry to
the Hôtel de Ville at Brussels; if Indigo Jones builds
an Italian Whitehall, Sir Christopher Wren builds an
Italian St. Paul's. But now you live under one school
of architecture, and worship under another. What do
you mean by doing this? Am I to understand that you
are thinking of changing your architecture back to
Gothic; and that you treat your churches experi-
mentally, because it does not matter what mistakes
you make in a church? Or am I to understand that
you consider Gothic a pre-eminently sacred and
beautiful mode of building, which you think, like the
fine frankincense, should be mixed for the tabernacle
only, and reserved for your religious services? For if
this be the feeling, though it may seem at first as if
it were graceful and reverent, at the root of the matter, it signifies neither more nor less than that you
have separated your religion from your life.

14. For consider what a wide significance this fact
has; and remember that it is not you only, but all the
people of England, who are behaving thus, just now.

15. You have all got into the habit of calling the
church "the house of God." I have seen, over the doors
of many churches, the legend actually carved, "*This
is the house of God and this is the gate of heaven.*" [4]
Now, note where the legend comes from, and of what
place it was first spoken. A boy leaves his father's
house to go on a long journey on foot, to visit his
uncle: he has to cross a wild hill-desert; just as if one
of your own boys had to cross the wolds to visit an
uncle at Carlisle. The second or third day your boy
finds himself somewhere between Hawes and Brough,
in the midst of the moors, at sunset. It is stony ground,

[4] Cf. Genesis 28:17.

and boggy; he cannot go one foot farther that night.
Down he lies, to sleep, on Wharnside, where best he
may, gathering a few of the stones together to put
under his head;—so wild the place is, he cannot get
anything but stones. And there, lying under the broad
night, he has a dream; and he sees a ladder set up on
the earth, and the top of it reaches to heaven, and the
angels of God are seen ascending and descending
upon it. And when he wakes out of his sleep, he says,
"How dreadful is this place; surely this is none other
than the house of God, and this is the gate of heaven."
This PLACE, observe; not this church; not this city;
not this stone, even, which he puts up for a memorial
—the piece of flint on which his head was lain. But
this *place;* this windy slope of Wharnside; this moor-
land hollow, torrent-bitten, snow-blighted! this *any*
place where God lets down the ladder. And how are
you to know where that will be? or how are you to
determine where it may be, but by being ready for it
always? Do you know where the lightning is to fall
next? You *do* know that, partly; you can guide the
lightning; but you cannot guide the going forth of
the Spirit, which is as that lightning when it shines
from the east to the west.[5]

16. But the perpetual and insolent warping of that
strong verse to serve a merely ecclesiastical purpose, is
only one of the thousand instances in which we sink
back into gross Judaism. We call our churches "temples." Now, you know perfectly well they are *not*
temples. They have never had, never can have, anything whatever to do with temples. They are "syna-
gogues"—"gathering places"—where you gather yourselves together as an assembly; and by not calling

[5] Cf. Matthew 24:27.

them so, you again miss the force of another mighty
text—"Thou, when thou prayest, shalt not be as the
hypocrites are; for they love to pray standing in the
churches [we should translate it],[6] "that they may be
seen of men. But thou, when thou prayest, enter into
thy closet, and when thou hast shut thy door, pray
to thy Father,"—which is, not in chancel nor in aisle,
but "in secret."[7]

17. Now, you feel, as I say this to you—I know you
feel—as if I were trying to take away the honor of
your churches. Not so; I am trying to prove to you
the honour of your houses and your hills; not that the
Church is not sacred—but that the whole Earth is. I
would have you feel what careless, what constant,
what infectious sin there is in all modes of thought,
whereby, in calling your churches only "holy," you
call your hearths and homes "profane"; and have
separated yourselves from the heathen by casting all
your household gods to the ground, instead of recognizing, in the places of their many and feeble Lares,[8]
the presence of your One and Mighty Lord and Lar.

18. "But what has all this to do with our Exchange?"
you ask me, impatiently. My dear friends, it has just
everything to do with it; on these inner and great
questions depend all the outer and little ones; and if
you have asked me down here to speak to you, because you had before been interested in anything I
have written, you must know that all I have yet said
about architecture was to show this. The book I
called *The Seven Lamps* was to show that certain right
states of temper and moral feeling were the magic

---

[6] Words within square brackets inserted by Ruskin in 1873.
[7] Cf. Matthew 6:6.
[8] Guardian spirits. Lar is the singular form.

powers by which all good architecture, without ex-
ception, had been produced. *The Stones of Venice*
had, from beginning to end, no other aim than to
show that the Gothic architecture of Venice had
arisen out of, and indicated in all its features, a state
of pure national faith, and of domestic virtue; and
that its Renaissance architecture had arisen out of,
and in all its features indicated, a state of concealed
national infidelity, and of domestic corruption. And
now, you ask me what style is best to build in, and
how can I answer, knowing the meaning of the two
styles but by another question—do you mean to build
as Christians or as infidels? And still more—do you
mean to build as honest Christians or as honest Infidels? as thoroughly and confessedly either one or the
other? You don't like to be asked such rude questions.
I cannot help it; they are of much more importance
than this Exchange business; and if they can be at
once answered, the Exchange business settles itself
in a moment. But before I press them farther, I must
ask leave to explain one point clearly.

19. In all my past work, my endeavour has been to
show that good architecture is essentially religious—
the production of a faithful and virtuous, not of an
infidel and corrupted people. But in the course of doing
this, I have had also to show that good architecture
is not *ecclesiastical*. People are so apt to look upon
religion as the business of the clergy, not their own,
that the moment they hear of anything depending on
"religion," they think it must also have depended on
the priesthood; and I have had to take what place was
to be occupied between these two errors, and fight
both, often with seeming contradiction. Good architecture is the work of good and believing men; there-

fore, you say, at least some people say, "Good architecture must essentially have been the work of the clergy, not of the laity." No—a thousand times no; good architecture has always been the work of the commonalty, *not* of the clergy. "What," you say, "those glorious cathedrals—the pride of Europe—did their builders not form Gothic architecture?" No; they corrupted Gothic architecture. Gothic was formed in the baron's castle, and the burgher's street. It was formed by the thoughts, and hands, and powers of labouring citizens and warrior kings. By the monk it was used as an instrument for the aid of his superstition: when that superstition became a beautiful madness, and the best hearts of Europe vainly dreamed and pined in the cloister, and vainly raged and perished in the crusade, —through that fury of perverted faith and wasted war, the Gothic rose also to its loveliest, most fantastic, and, finally, most foolish dreams; and in those dreams was lost.

20. I hope, now, that there is no risk of your misunderstanding me when I come to the gist of what I want to say to-night;—when I repeat, that every great national architecture has been the result and exponent of a great national religion. You can't have bits of it here, bits there—you must have it everywhere or nowhere. It is not the monopoly of a clerical company— it is not the exponent of a theological dogma—it is not the hieroglyphic writing of an initiated priesthood; it is the manly language of a people inspired by resolute and common purpose, and rendering resolute and common fidelity to the legible laws of an undoubted God.

21. Now there have as yet been three distinct schools of European architecture. I say, European, because

Asiatic and African architectures belong so entirely to other races and climates, that there is no question of them here; only, in passing, I will simply assure you that whatever is good or great in Egypt, and Syria, and India, is just good or great for the same reasons as the buildings on our side of the Bosphorus. We Europeans, then, have had three great religions: the Greek, which was the worship of the God of Wisdom and Power; the Mediaeval, which was the worship of the God of Judgment and Consolation; the Renaissance, which was the worship of the God of Pride and Beauty: these three we have had—they are past,— and now, at last, we English have got a fourth religion, and a God of our own, about which I want to ask you. But I must explain these three old ones first.

22. I repeat, first, the Greeks essentially worshipped the God of Wisdom; so that whatever contended against their religion,—to the Jews a stumbling-block, —was, to the Greeks—*Foolishness*.[9]

23. The first Greek idea of deity was that expressed in the word, of which we keep the remnant in our words "*Di*-urnal" and "*Di*-vine"—the god of *Day*, Jupiter the revealer. Athena is his daughter, but especially daughter of the Intellect, springing armed from the head. We are only with the help of recent investigation beginning to penetrate the depth of meaning couched under the Athenaic symbols: but I may note rapidly, that her aegis, the mantle with the serpent fringes, in which she often, in the best statues, is represented as folding up her left hand, for better guard; and the Gorgon, on her shield, are both representative mainly of the chilling horror and sadness

[9] Cf. I Corinthians 1:23.

(turning men to stone, as it were,) of the outmost and superficial spheres of knowledge—that knowledge which separates, in bitterness, hardness, and sorrow, the heart of the full-grown man from the heart of the child. For out of imperfect knowledge spring terror, dissension, danger, and disdain; but from perfect knowledge, given by the full-revealed Athena, strength and peace, in sign of which she is crowned with the olive spray, and bears the resistless spear.

24. This, then, was the Greek conception of purest Deity; and every habit of life, and every form of his art developed themselves from the seeking this bright, serene, resistless wisdom; and setting himself, as a man, to do things evermore rightly and strongly; not with any ardent affection or ultimate hope; but with a resolute and continent energy of will, as knowing that for failure there was no consolation, and for sin there was no remission. And the Greek architecture rose unerring, bright, clearly defined, and self-contained.

25. Next followed in Europe the great Christian faith, which was essentially the religion of Comfort. Its great doctrine is the remission of sins; for which cause, it happens, too often, in certain phases of Christianity, that sin and sickness themselves are partly glorified, as if, the more you had to be healed of, the more divine was the healing. The practical result of this doctrine, in art, is a continual contemplation of sin and disease, and of imaginary states of purification from them; thus we have an architecture conceived in a mingled sentiment of melancholy and aspiration, partly severe, partly luxuriant, which will bend itself to every one of our needs, and every one of our fancies, and be strong or weak with us, as we

are strong or weak ourselves. It is, of all architecture, the basest, when base people build it—of all, the noblest, when built by the noble.

26. And now note that both these religions—Greek and Mediaeval—perished by falsehood in their own main purpose. The Greek religion of Wisdom perished in a false philosophy—"Oppositions of science, falsely so called." [10] The Mediaeval religion of Consolation perished in false comfort; in remission of sins given lyingly. It was the selling of absolution that ended the Mediaeval faith; and I can tell you more, it is the selling of absolution which, to the end of time, will mark false Christianity. Pure Christianity gives her remission of sins only by *ending* them; but false Christianity gets her remission of sins by *compounding for* them. And there are many ways of compounding for them. We English have beautiful little quiet ways of buying absolution, whether in low Church or high, far more cunning than any of Tetzel's trading. [11]

27. Then, thirdly, there followed the religion of Pleasure, in which all Europe gave itself to luxury, ending in death. First, *bals masqués* in every saloon, and then guillotines in every square. And all these three worships issue in vast temple building. Your Greek worshipped Wisdom, and built you the Parthenon—the Virgin's temple. The Mediaeval worshipped Consolation, and built you Virgin temples also—but to our Lady of Salvation. Then the Revivalist worshipped beauty, of a sort, and built you Versailles and

[10] Cf. I Timothy 6:20.
[11] Johann Tetzel whose attitude towards the selling of Indulgences was a partial motivation for Luther's nailing of his *theses* on the door of the church at Wittenberg.

the Vatican. Now, lastly, will you tell me what *we* worship, and what *we* build?

28. You know we are speaking always of the real, active, continual, national worship; that by which men act, while they live; not that which they talk of, when they die. Now, we have, indeed, a nominal religion, to which we pay tithes of property and sevenths of time; but we have also a practical and earnest religion, to which we devote nine-tenths of our property, and six-sevenths of our time. And we dispute a great deal about the nominal religion: but we are all unanimous about this practical one; of which I think you will admit that the ruling goddess may be best described as the "Goddess of Getting-on," or "Britannia of the Market." The Athenians had an "Athena Agoraia," or Athena of the Market; but she was a subordinate type of their goddess, while our Britannia Agoraia is the principal type of ours. And all your great architectural works are, of course, built to her. It is long since you built a great cathedral; and how you would laugh at me if I proposed building a cathedral on the top of one of these hills of yours, to make it an Acropolis! But your railroad mounds, vaster than the walls of Babylon; your railroad stations, vaster than the temple of Ephesus, and innumerable; your chimneys, how much more mighty and costly than cathedral spires! your harbour-piers; your warehouses; your exchanges! —all these are built to your great Goddess of "Getting-on"; and she has formed, and will continue to form, your architecture, as long as you worship her; and it is quite vain to ask me to tell you how to build to *her*; you know far better than I.

29. There might, indeed, on some theories, be a

conceivably good architecture for Exchanges—that is
to say, if there were any heroism in the fact or deed
of exchange, which might be typically carved on the
outside of your building. For, you know, all beautiful
architecture must be adorned with sculpture or painting; and for sculpture or painting, you must have a
subject. And hitherto it has been a received opinion
among the nations of the world that the only right
subjects for either, were *heroisms* of some sort. Even
on his pots and his flagons, the Greek put a Hercules
slaying lions, or an Apollo slaying serpents, or Bacchus slaying melancholy giants, and earthborn de-
spondencies. On his temples, the Greek put contests
of great warriors in founding states, or of gods with
evil spirits. On his houses and temples alike, the
Christian put carvings of angels conquering devils; or
of hero-martyrs exchanging this world for another:
subject inappropriate, I think, to our direction of exchange here. And the Master of Christians not only
left His followers without any orders as to the sculpture of affairs of exchange on the outside of buildings,
but gave some strong evidence of His dislike of affairs
of exchange within them.[12] And yet there might surely
be a heroism in such affairs; and all commerce become
a kind of selling of doves, not impious. The wonder
has always been great to me, that heroism has never
been supposed to be in anywise consistent with the
practice of supplying people with food, or clothes; but
rather with that of quartering one's self upon them
for food, and stripping them of their clothes. Spoiling
of armour is an heroic deed in all ages; but the selling
of clothes, old, or new, has never taken any colour of

[12] Cf. Matthew 21:12ff.

magnanimity. Yet one does not see why feeding the
hungry and clothing the naked should ever become
base businesses, even, when engaged in on a large
scale. If one could contrive to attach the notion of
conquest to them anyhow! so that, supposing there
were anywhere an obstinate race, who refused to be
comforted, one might take some pride in giving them
compulsory comfort! and, as it were, "*occupying* a
country" with one's gifts, instead of one's armies? If
one could only consider it as much a victory to get a
barren field sown, as to get an eared field stripped;
and contend who should build villages, instead of who
should "carry" them! Are not all forms of heroism
conceivable in doing these serviceable deeds? You
doubt who is strongest? It might be ascertained by
push of spade, as well as push of sword. Who is wisest?
There are witty things to be thought of in planning
other business than campaigns. Who is bravest? There
are always the elements to fight with, stronger than
men; and nearly as merciless.

30. The only absolutely and unapproachably heroic
element in the soldier's work seems to be—that he is
paid little for it—and regularly: while you traffickers,
and exchangers, and others occupied in presumably
benevolent business, like to be paid much for it—and
by chance. I never can make out how it is that a
knight-errant does not expect to be paid for his trouble,
but a *pedlar*-errant always does;—that people are
willing to take hard knocks for nothing, but never to
sell ribands cheap; that they are ready to go on fervent
crusades, to recover the tomb of a buried God, but
never on any travels to fulfil the orders of a living
one;—that they will go anywhere barefoot to preach

their faith, but must be well bribed to practise it, and are perfectly ready to give the Gospel gratis, but never the loaves and fishes.

31. If you chose to take the matter up on any such soldierly principle; to do your commerce, and your feeding of nations, for fixed salaries; and to be as particular about giving people the best food, and the best cloth, as soldiers are about giving them the best gunpowder, I could carve something for you on your exchange worth looking at. But I can only at present suggest decorating its frieze with pendant purses; and making its pillars broad at the base, for the sticking of bills. And in the innermost chambers of it there might be a statue of Britannia of the Market, who may have, perhaps advisably, a partridge for her crest, typical at once of her courage in fighting for noble ideas, and of her interest in game; and round its neck, the inscription in golden letters, "Perdix fovit quae non peperit." [13] Then, for her spear, she might have a weaver's beam; and on her shield, instead of St. George's Cross, the Milanese boar, semi-fleeced, with the town of Gennesaret proper, in the field; and the legend, "In the best market," and her corslet, of leather, folded over her heart in the shape of a purse, with thirty slits in it, for a piece of money to go in at, on each day of the month. And I doubt not but that people would come to see your exchange, and its goddess, with applause.

32. Nevertheless, I want to point out to you certain strange characters in this goddess of yours. She differs

[13] "The partridge fostered that which it did not bring forth." But essentially to the point is Jeremiah 17:11 where the partridge figure is part of a moral reflection on riches.

from the great Greek and Mediaeval deities essentially in two things—first, as to the continuance of her presumed power; secondly, as to the extent of it.

33. 1st, as to the Continuance.

34. The Greek Goddess of Wisdom gave continual increase of wisdom, as the Christian Spirit of Comfort (or Comforter) continual increase of comfort. There was no question, with these, of any limit or cessation of function. But with your Agora Goddess, that is just the most important question. Getting on— but where to? Gathering together—but how much? Do you mean to gather always—never to spend? If so, I wish you joy of your goddess, for I am just as well off as you, without the trouble of worshipping her at all. But if you do not spend, somebody else will— somebody else must. And it is because of this (among many other such errors) that I have fearlessly declared your so-called science of Political Economy to be no science; because, namely, it has omitted the study of exactly the most important branch of the business— the study of *spending*. For spend you must, and as much as you make, ultimately. You gather corn:— will you bury England under a heap of grain; or will you, when you have gathered, finally eat? You gather gold:—will you make your house-roofs of it, or pave your streets with it? That is still one way of spending it. But if you keep it, that you may get more, I'll give you more; I'll give you all the gold you want— all you can imagine—if you can tell me what you'll do with it. You shall have thousands of gold pieces;— thousand of thousands—millions—mountains, of gold: where will you keep them? Will you put an Olympus of silver upon a golden Pelion—make Ossa like a

wart? [14] Do you think the rain and dew would then
come down to you, in the streams from such mountains, more blessedly than they will down the mountains which God has made for you, of moss and
whinstone? But it is not gold that you want to gather!
What is it? greenbacks? No; not those neither. What
is it then—is it ciphers after a capital I? Cannot you
practise writing ciphers, and write as many as you
want! Write ciphers for an hour every morning, in
a big book, and say every evening, I am worth all
those noughts more than I was yesterday. Won't that
do? Well, what in the name of Plutus is it you want?
Not gold, not greenbacks, not ciphers after a capital I?
You will have to answer, after all, "No; we want,
somehow or other, money's *worth*." Well, what is that?
Let your Goddess of Getting-on discover it, and let
her learn to stay therein.

35. II. But there is yet another question to be asked
respecting this Goddess of Getting-on. The first was
of the continuance of her power; the second is of
its extent.

36. Pallas and the Madonna were supposed to be
all the world's Pallas, and all the world's Madonna.
They could teach all men, and they could comfort
all men. But, look strictly into the nature of the power
of your Goddess of Getting-on; and you will find she
is the Goddess—not of everybody's getting on—but
only of somebody's getting on. This is a vital, or rather
deathful, distinction. Examine it in your own ideal
of the state of national life which this Goddess is to
evoke and maintain. I asked you what it was, when I

[14] This image, evocative of the assault of the giants upon
the gods, is designed to criticize superfluous accumulation of
wealth.

was last here;—you have never told me. Now, shall
I try to tell you?

37. Your ideal of human life then is, I think, that
it should be passed in a pleasant undulating world,
with iron and coal everywhere underneath it. On
each pleasant bank of this world is to be a beautiful
mansion, with two wings; and stables, and coach-
houses; a moderately-sized park; a large garden and
hot-houses; and pleasant carriage drives through the
shrubberies. In this mansion are to live the favoured
votaries of the Goddess; the English gentleman, with
his gracious wife, and his beautiful family; he always
able to have the boudoir and the jewels for the wife,
and the beautiful ball dresses for the daughters, and
hunters for the sons, and a shooting in the Highlands
for himself. At the bottom of the bank, is to be the
mill; not less than a quarter of a mile long, with one
steam engine at each end, and two in the middle, and
a chimney three hundred feet high. In this mill are
to be in constant employment from eight hundred to
a thousand workers, who never drink, never strike,
always go to church on Sunday, and always express
themselves in respectful language.

38. Is not that, broadly, and in the main features,
the kind of thing you propose to yourselves? It is
very pretty indeed, seen from above; not at all so
pretty, seen from below. For, observe, while to one
family this deity is indeed the Goddess of Getting-on,
to a thousand families she is the Goddess of *not* Getting-on. "Nay," you say, "they have all their chance."
Yes, so has every one in a lottery, but there must
always be the same number of blanks. "Ah! but in
a lottery it is not skill and intelligence which take the
lead, but blind chance." What then! do you think

the old practice, that "they should take who have the power, and they should keep who can," [15] is less iniquitous, when the power has become power of brains instead of fist? and that, though we may not take advantage of a child's or a woman's weakness, we may of a man's foolishness? "Nay, but finally, work must be done, and some one must be at the top, some one at the bottom." Granted, my friends. Work must always be, and captains of work must always be; and if you in the least remember the tone of any of my writings, you must know that they are thought unfit for this age, because they are always insisting on need of government, and speaking with scorn of liberty. But I beg you to observe that there is a wide difference between being captains or governors of work, and taking the profits of it.[16] It does not follow, because you are general of an army, that you are to take all the treasure, or land, it wins; (if it fight for treasure or land;) neither, because you are king of a nation, that you are to consume all the profits of the nation's work. Real kings on the contrary, are known invariably by their doing quite the reverse of this,—by their taking the least possible quantity of the nation's work for themselves. There is no test of real kinghood so infallible as that. Does the crowned creature live simply, bravely, unostentatiously? probably he *is* a King. Does he cover his body with jewels, and his table with delicates? in all probability he is *not* a King. It is possible he may be, as Solomon was; but that is when the nation shares his splendour with him. Solomon made gold, not only to be in his own

[15] Cf. Wordsworth "Rob Roy's Grave" stanza ix.
[16] One of numerous echoes of Carlyle's beliefs.

palace as stones, but to be in Jerusalem as stones.[17]
But, even so, for the most part, these splendid kinghoods expire in ruin, and only the true kinghoods live,
which are of royal labourers governing loyal labourers;
who, both leading rough lives, establish the true dy-
nasties. Conclusively you will find that because you
are king of a nation, it does not follow that you are
to gather for yourself all the wealth of that nation;
neither, because you are king of a small part of the
nation, and lord over the means of its maintenance—
over field, or mill, or mine,—are you to take all the
produce of that piece of the foundation of national
existence for yourself.

39. You will tell me I need not preach against
these things, for I cannot mend them. No, good
friends, I cannot; but you can, and you will; or something else can and will. Even good things have no
abiding power—and shall these evil things persist in
victorious evil? All history shows, on the contrary,
that to be the exact thing they never can do. Change
must come; but it is ours to determine whether change
of growth, or change of death. Shall the Parthenon
be in ruins on its rock, and Bolton priory in its
meadow, but these mills of yours be the consummation
of the buildings of the earth, and their wheels be as
the wheels of eternity? Think you that "men may
come, and men may go," [18] but—mills—go on for ever?
Not so; out of these, better or worse shall come; and
it is for you to choose which.

40. I know that none of this wrong is done with
deliberate purpose. I know, on the contrary, that you

[17] I Kings 10:27.
[18] Cf. Tennyson's "The Brook."

wish your workmen well; that you do much for them, and that you desire to do more for them, if you saw your way to such benevolence safely. I know that even all this wrong and misery are brought about by a warped sense of duty, each of you striving to do his best; but, unhappily, not knowing for whom this best should be done. And all our hearts have been betrayed by the plausible impiety of the modern economist, telling us that, "To do the best for ourselves, is finally to do the best for others." Friends, our great Master said not so; and most absolutely we shall find this world is not made so. Indeed, to do the best for others, is finally to do the best for ourselves; but it will not do to have our eyes fixed on that issue. The Pagans had got beyond that. Hear what a Pagan says of this matter; hear what were, perhaps, the last written words of Plato,—if not the last actually written (for this we cannot know), yet assuredly in fact and power his parting words—in which, endeavouring to give full crowning and harmonious close to all his thoughts, and to speak the sum of them by the imagined sentence of the Great Spirit, his strength and his heart fail him, and the words cease, broken off for ever.

41. They are at the close of the dialogue called *Critias*, in which he describes, partly from real tradition, partly in ideal dream, the early state of Athens; and the genesis, and order, and religion, of the fabled isle of Atlantis; in which genesis he conceives the same first perfection and final degeneracy of man, which in our own Scriptural tradition is expressed by saying that the Sons of God inter-married with the daughters of men,[19] for he supposes the earliest race

[19] Cf. Genesis 6:2.

to have been indeed the children of God; and to have
corrupted themselves, until "their spot was not the
spot of his children." [20] And this, he says, was the
end; that indeed [21] "through many generations, so
long as the God's nature in them yet was full, they
were submissive to the sacred laws, and carried themselves lovingly to all that had kindred with them in
divineness; for their uttermost spirit was faithful and
true, and in every wise great; so that, in *all meekness
of wisdom, they dealt with each other,* and took all
the chances of life; and despising all things except
virtue, they cared little what happened day by day,
and *bore lightly the burden* of gold and of possessions;
for they saw that, if *only their common love and virtue
increased, all these things would be increased together
with them;* but to set their esteem and ardent pursuit
upon material possession would be to lose that first,
and their virtue and affection together with it. And by
such reasoning, and what of the divine nature remained in them, they gained all this greatness of
which we have already told; but when the God's part
of them faded and became extinct, being mixed again
and again, and effaced by the prevalent mortality; and
the human nature at last exceeded, they then became
unable to endure the courses of fortune; and fell into
shapelessness of life, and baseness in the sight of him
who could see, having lost everything that was fairest
of their honour; while to the blind hearts which could
not discern the true life, tending to happiness, it
seemed that they were then chiefly noble and happy,
being filled with all iniquity of inordinate possession

---

[20] Cf. Deuteronomy 32:5.
[21] From here to the end of the paragraph Ruskin offers his own
interpretation of the concluding passages of the *Critias.*

and power. Whereupon, the God of Gods, whose
Kinghood is in laws, beholding a once just nation
thus cast into misery, and desiring to lay such punish-
ment upon them as might make them repent into
restraining, gathered together all the gods into his
dwelling place, which from heaven's centre overlooks
whatever has part in creation; and having assembled
them, he said"—

42. The rest is silence.[22] Last words of the chief
wisdom of the heathen, spoken of this idol of riches;
this idol of yours; this golden image, high by measure-
less cubits,[23] set up where your green fields of England
are furnace-burnt into the likeness of the plain of
Dura:[24] this idol, forbidden to us, first of all idols,
by our own Master and faith; forbidden to us also by
every human lip that has ever, in any age or people,
been accounted of as able to speak according to the
purposes of God. Continue to make that forbidden
deity your principal one, and soon no more art, no
more science, no more pleasure will be possible. Catastrophe will come; or, worse than catastrophe, slow
mouldering and withering into Hades. But if you can
fix some conception of a true human state of life to
be striven for—life, good for all men, as for yourselves; if you can determine some honest and simple
order of existence; following those trodden ways of
wisdom, which are pleasantness, and seeking her quiet
and withdrawn paths, which are peace;[25]—then, and
so sanctifying wealth into "commonwealth," all your
art, your literature, your daily labours, your domestic

[22] Hamlet's final words.
[23] Cf. Daniel 3:1.
[24] *Ibid.*
[25] Cf. Proverbs 3:17.

affection, and citizen's duty, will join and increase
into one magnificent harmony. You will know then
how to build, well enough; you will build with stone
well, but with flesh better; temples not made with
hands,[26] but riveted of hearts; and that kind of marble,
crimson-veined, is indeed eternal.

[26] Cf. Acts 7:48.

SELECTED BIBLIOGRAPHY

WRITINGS

The Works of John Ruskin, edited by E. T. Cook and
Alexander Wedderburn (39 vols., London, 1903-
1912). Handsomely illustrated and copiously an-
notated, this complete edition of Ruskin's works
(including two volumes of letters and a bibliography
extending to 1911) should nevertheless be consulted
with reservation because of its numerous minor
slips and inaccuracies.

*The Order of Release: The Story of John Ruskin,
Effie Gray, and John Everett Millais told for the
first time in their unpublished letters,* edited by
Admiral Sir William James (London, 1947). A
sharply prejudiced epistolary account—indifferently
edited—of Ruskin's fervent courtship and ill-fated
marriage.

Selected Writings of John Ruskin, edited and introduced by Peter Quennell (London, 1952). The most
sensible and useful general introduction to the scope
and significance of Ruskin's writings marred, occa-
sionally, by omissions within individual selections.

Ruskin's Letters from Venice 1851-52, edited by John L.
Bradley (New Haven, 1955). Letters to his father
written while preparing *The Stones of Venice II, III.*
Of interest as illuminating his methods of working.

The Diaries of John Ruskin, selected and edited by
   Joan Evans and J. Howard Whitehouse (Oxford,
   1956-1959). A carelessly edited account of much
   of Ruskin's daily life between 1835 and 1889. To be
   used with discretion.

The Genius of John Ruskin, edited with an introduction
   by John D. Rosenberg (New York, 1963). Selections
   which tend to stress Ruskin's best known writings.

Ruskin Today, edited by Sir Kenneth Clark (London,
   1964). Excerpts from Ruskin's writings grouped
   under six headings: Self-Portrait, Nature, Art, Architecture, Society and Economics, Poetic Descrip-
   tion. The brevity of the selections precludes awareness of the majestic movement of Ruskin's prose;
   and biographically the volume is not satisfactory.

The Art Criticism of John Ruskin, selected, edited,
   and with an introduction by R. L. Herbert (New
   York, 1964). A commendable attempt to bring order
   out of the mass of Ruskin's art criticism.

*The Letters of John Ruskin to Lord and Lady Mount-
   Temple,* edited by John L. Bradley (Columbus,
   Ohio, 1964). A correspondence concerning Ruskin's
   disastrous relationship with Rose La Touche and
   indirectly suggestive of her influence upon his later
   writings.

The Literary Criticism of John Ruskin, edited and
   with an introduction by Harold Bloom (New York,
   1965). Preceded by an introduction not wholly
   free from biographical error, this aggregation, chron-
   ologically arranged, reveals Ruskin's extraordinarily
   wide and perceptive powers as a literary critic.

Numerous other volumes of Ruskin's correspondence
as well as selections from his works have been assem-

bled over the years. Most are spoiled—in the case of letters by numerous editorial inaccuracies and in the case of selections, by salient omissions from within the works themselves.

BIOGRAPHY AND CRITICISM

The Art Teaching of John Ruskin, by W. G. Collingwood (London, 1891). A useful guide to various aspects of Ruskin's thought.

The Life and Work of John Ruskin, by W. G. Collingwood (2 vols., London, 1893). Perhaps the most sophisticated of the earlier studies.

John Ruskin, by Frederic Harrison (London, 1902). A sound general and succinct account of Ruskin's life and major writings.

The Life of Ruskin, by E. T. Cook (2 vols., London, 1911). Most of the matter of this study derives from the introductions to the various volumes comprising the *Works*.

Ruskin: a Study in Personality, by A. C. Benson (London, 1911). Seven lectures stressing the man rather than his work.

Ruskin's Politics, by Bernard Shaw (London, 1921). A witty disquisition on Ruskin's Tory-Socialism.

The Victorian Morality of Art, by Henry Ladd (New York, 1932). Turgidly written, this book is an heroic and frequently successful attempt to clarify Ruskin's complex aesthetic.

John Ruskin, by R. H. Wilenski (London, 1933). A provocative analysis of Ruskin's mentality.

John Ruskin, by Peter Quennell (London, 1949). An urbanely written study emphasizing Ruskin's amatory difficulties.

The Last Romantics, by Graham Hough (London 1949). The initial essay, on Ruskin, is an excellent introduction to his aesthetic; his relationship to the visual is well developed.

Ruskin: The Great Victorian, by Derrick Leon (London, 1949). The most searching, comprehensive, and perceptive study of the man and his work written to date.

The Captain's Death Bed, by Virginia Woolf (London, 1950). Her essay, "Ruskin," communicates more in a few hundred words than many a lengthy treatise.

Ruskin's Scottish Heritage, by Helen Gill Viljoen (Urbana, Illinois, 1956). A detailed and significant account of Ruskin's background, this book reveals endless new facts about his ancestry and corrects many long perpetuated errors.

Ruskin and the Economists, by John Tyree Fain (Nashville, Tennessee, 1956). An excellent short discussion of Ruskin's political economy; the book includes a sound chapter on *Unto this Last.*

Ruskin, by Quentin Bell (Edinburgh, 1963). Possibly the best short introduction to Ruskin now available.

The Darkening Glass, by John Rosenberg (London, 1963). Floridly written and not infrequently dogmatic, this book is nevertheless notable for its sensitivity toward Ruskin and his major writings.

Effie in Venice, by Mary Lutyens (London, 1965). Letters written by Effie Ruskin in 1849-50 and 1851-52 which, while yielding little new about her husband, form a delightful picture of Venetian society of the time.